Diamond Ring Buying Guide

How to evaluate, identify and select diamonds & diamond jewelry

Sixth Edition

Platinum bridal rings from Joey Clapper
Photo from Wright and Lato

Diamond Ring Buying Guide

How to evaluate, identify and select diamonds & diamond jewelry

Sixth Edition

Renée Newman

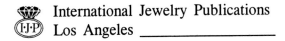
International Jewelry Publications
Los Angeles _____

S

International Jewelry Publications
P.O. Box 13384
Los Angeles, CA 90013-0384 USA

(Inquiries should be accompanied by a self-addressed, stamped envelope).

Printed in Singapore

Library of Congress Cataloging in Publication Data

Newman, Renée
    Diamond ring buying guide: How to evaluate, identify and select diamonds & diamond jewelry / text & photographs by Renée Newman. — 6th ed.
        p. cm.
    Includes bibliographical references and index.
    ISBN 0-929975-32-4 (paperback : alk. paper)
    1. Diamonds—Purchasing. 2. Rings—Purchasing. I. Title.

TS753 .N47 2002
736'.23'0297—dc21

                              2001026393

Rings and photo on front cover from Varna Platinum,
Los Angeles, CA
Photo & ring on title page from Judith Conway, Windsor, CA

To Bill

If it weren't for him, none of my books would have been written. Bill encouraged me to become a tour director and taught me how to do it; and then when I was exposed to a wide array of gems on tours abroad, I developed an interest in gemology. While I was a tour director, my passengers wanted me to explain how to judge the quality of the gems they saw. This was when I realized there was a need for books on how to buy and evaluate gems. It's taken a long time for me to gain the gemological background and trade experience required to write my gem books, but the entire journey has been fun, absorbing and exhilarating.

Thanks Bill for the wonderful careers to which you've led me and for all your support along the way.

Contents

Acknowledgments

I would like to express my appreciation to the following people for their contribution to the *Diamond Ring Buying Guide*:

Ernie and Regina Goldberger of the Josam Diamond Trading Corporation. This book could never have been written without the experience and knowledge I gained from working with them. A large percentage of the loose diamonds pictured in this book are or were part of their collection.

Chuck Atmore, Daniel Ballard, Christopher J. Cart, Judith Conway, Gary Dulac, Patricia Esparza, Elaine Ferrari-Santhon, Michael Francis, Sean Hagens, Laurie A. Hudson, Susan B. Johnson, Douglas Kato, Krista Kuether, Joe Landau, Arthur Langerman, Jurgen Maerz, Peter Malnekoff, Garbis Mazmanian, Marian Newton, Carlos Pulido, Howard Rubin, Cassie Saget, Sindi Schloss, Kathrin Schoenke, Dr. James E. Shigley, Peter Solomon, Dale Swanson, Tom Tashey and Eric Walls. They have made valuable suggestions, corrections and comments regarding the portions of the book they examined. They are not responsible for any possible errors, nor do they necessarily endorse the material contained in this book.

The teachers at the GIA. They helped me obtain the technical background needed to write a book such as this. Their dedication and assistance extend well beyond class hours.

Ebert & Company, Patricia Esparza, Douglas Kato, J. Landau, Inc., Lisa Poff, Rainbow G. I. Diamonds, Ralph Shapiro, Marge Vaughn and the Yehuda Diamond Co. Their stones or jewelry have been used for some of the photographs.

A.I.G.S., Eve Alfillé, Ambar Diamonds, Inc., Zsombor Antal, Michael Bondanza, Christopher Designs, Judith Conway, Gary Dulac, Ebert & Company, Extrême Gioielli, Michael Francis, Dr. Ulrich Freisleben, Gemological Institute of America, Global Diamonds, Inc., Mary V. Hall, Aaron Henry Designs, Alan Hodgkinson, Scott Keating, Richard Kimball, J. Landau, Inc., Arthur Langerman, Wade Miley, Sidney Mobell, Nagalle Designs, Platinum Guild International USA, Todd Reed, Cynthia Renée, Andrew Sarosi, Mark Schneider, Peter Storm Designs, Studio E, Stuller, Suberi Bros., Suna Bros. Inc., Timeless Gem Designs, Varna Platinum, Vivid Collection, Walls Design, Harry Winston, Inc., Wright & Lato, and the Yehuda Diamond Co. Photos and/or diagrams from them have been reproduced in this book.

Greg Hatfield, Ion Itescu, Don Nelson and Avery Osborne. They've provided technical assistance.

Louise Harris Berlin. She has spent hours carefully editing the *Diamond Ring Buying Guide*. Thanks to her, this book is much easier for consumers to read and understand.

My sincere thanks to all of these contributors for their kindness and help.

Preface

When the *Diamond Ring Buying Guide* was first published in 1989, it was the only book on the market that gave detailed guidelines on how to select a diamond ring. The book has stood the test of time. In fact, it's even more popular today than when it first came out. That doesn't mean, though, it shouldn't be improved.

In response to requests from readers and to new trends in the diamond and jewelry market, the following changes have been made in this new Sixth Edition:

♦ There are many more photographs and examples of diamond rings and most of the previous photographs of rings have been updated.

♦ Forty-six photos of unset diamonds have been added. New cutting styles are shown and more photos of diamond clarity are included. Overall the book is more colorful.

♦ The chapter on diamond color has been expanded to include more information and photos on fancy color diamonds. Fancy colors are more popular and available now than in 1996 when the Fifth Edition was published.

♦ New information and tables have been added to the chapter on judging cut quality.

♦ Photos and detection guidelines for synthetic moissanite have been added. This new diamond imitation was not mentioned in the first three printings of the Fifth Edition.

♦ The chapter previously entitled "Fracture-Filled Diamonds" has been rewritten and is now entitled "Diamond Treatments." New treatments have appeared since the Fifth Edition was published and they're more widespread.

♦ The chapters on gold and platinum have been combined so the two metals can be more clearly compared. New information and photos have been added.

♦ New setting and ring styles are discussed and illustrated.

♦ There's a new first chapter entitled "Diamond Price Factors in a Nutshell" in which I explain why the 4 C's is not an adequate pricing system. In my opinion, consumers must also consider the two T's of *transparency* and *treatment status* if they expect to get a good buy.

In addition, I think it's better if shape and cut quality are identified as two separate price factors. The diamond trade treats them as separate factors, and it's easier for consumers to understand how they affect price if they're presented separately.

My goal is to help you select a ring that will bring you continuous pleasure and last a lifetime. Buying a diamond ring is a special event. Learn to ask the right questions so you'll be able to make smart choices and turn this event into a completely positive experience.

1

Diamond Price Factors in a Nutshell

There are seven basic price factors for diamonds:

♦ **Cut quality** (Proportions and finish)
♦ **Color**
♦ **Carat weight**
♦ **Clarity** (Degree to which a stone is free from flaws)
♦ **Cutting style & stone shape**
♦ **Transparency**
♦ **Treatment status** (Untreated or treated? What type of treatment?)

Why the 4 C's is Not an Adequate Pricing System

You may be surprised that there are more than four price factors if you've heard about the 4 C's of color, cut, clarity and carat weight. The 4 C's system of valuing gems is a clever, convenient way to explain gem pricing. The problem is that it causes consumers to overlook the importance of cut quality, treatment status and transparency.

If you see a mini gem-lab report stating that the shape/cut of a diamond is round brilliant, you may assume that this tells you everything about the cut of stone when in fact it doesn't. The quality of the cut is important and it's a separate price factor from shape and cutting style.

If you're not informed about gem treatments, you may assume, for example, that two equally attractive diamonds should be priced alike. However, if one is fracture-filled or irradiated and the other is untreated, their prices should be quite different.

If you're comparing a cloudy stone to a transparent one, be aware that transparency can have a significant impact on each stone's value. Transparency and clarity are often interconnected, but they're not the same. A stone can be transparent like crystal, yet have a low clarity. Likewise a gem may be flawless, yet be translucent. See Chapter 7 for more information on transparency.

In short, smart diamond buyers will consider the 5 C's and 2 T's instead of just the 4 C's.

Price Factors Explained

CUT QUALITY: (Proportions and finish, also called **make**): This is a crucial factor which can affect prices by as much as 50%. Two of the main considerations of cut are:

1. **Do you see brilliance all across the stone when you look at the diamond face up** (fig. 1.1)? Diamond brilliance should not be interrupted by white circular or dark areas (figs 1.3–1.5).
2. **Are you paying for excess weight?** (fig. 1.6)

Judge cut with the unaided eye and a 10X magnifier. Chapter 6 explains cut evaluation in detail.

Fig. 1.1 Well-cut diamond

Fig. 1.2 Profile of diamond in fig. 1.1

Fig. 1.3 White circle (fisheye) in a diamond with a poor quality cut

Fig. 1.4 A dark center in a diamond with poor proportions.

Fig. 1.5 Diamond with a dark center shaped like a bow tie.

Fig. 1.6 Diamond with excess weight

COLOR: Basically the less color, the higher the price (except for fancy colors). Stones that are as clear as colorless water are the most expensive and have a D to F rating, D being the highest. As the letters descend towards Z, more color is present. See the GIA (Gemological Institute of America) color grading scale below. Brown and gray diamonds are graded on the same scale.

<u>D E F*</u>	<u>G H I J</u>	<u>K L M</u>	<u>N</u> to <u>Z</u>	<u>Z +</u>
colorless	near colorless	faint yellow	very light–light yellow	fancy yellow

(*Colorless for 0.50 ct or less, near colorless for heavier stones)

A diamond is not bad quality just because it's yellowish. It's simply worth less because there's a higher demand and lower supply of natural colorless diamonds.

Diamonds with a natural body color other than light yellow, light brown or light gray are called **fancy color diamonds**. These colored diamonds may cost a lot more than those which are colorless. For example, a one-carat natural pink diamond could sell for five to fifteen times more than a D color diamond of the same size and quality.

Some diamonds are colored artificially by irradiation or high-pressure high-temperature treatment. They're worth significantly less than natural color diamonds. In the GIA system, treated colored diamonds are not considered fancy diamonds. But in the trade, they're sometimes referred to as "treated (enhanced or processed) fancy diamonds."

Fig. 1.7 Diamonds of five different color grades ranging from D (colorless) to Z (light yellow). Actual colors are a little different than printed colors. *Photo and diamonds from J. Landau, Inc.*

CARAT WEIGHT: In most cases, the higher the carat weight category, the greater the per-carat price of the diamond. A carat is a unit of weight equalling 1/5 of a gram. The weight of small diamonds is frequently expressed in points, with one point equaling 0.01 carats.

There is a difference between the labels **1 ct TW** (one carat total weight) and **1 ct** (the weight of one stone). A ring with a **1 ct** top quality diamond can be worth more than 10 times as much as a ring with 1 ct TW of diamonds of the same quality.

CLARITY: The fewer, smaller and less noticeable the flaws, the higher the price. There are 11 GIA clarity grades. They are:

Fl: Flawless—no **inclusions** (flaws inside the diamond) and no **blemishes** (flaws on the surface).

IF: Internally Flawless—no inclusions and only insignificant blemishes

VVS$_1$ & VVS$_2$: Very, very slightly included—minute flaws difficult to see with a 10X magnifier.

VS$_1$ & VS$_2$: Very slightly included—minor inclusions ranging from difficult to somewhat easy to see under 10-power magnification.

SI$_1$ & SI$_2$: Slightly included, noticeable inclusions easy (SI$_1$) or very easy (SI$_2$) to see under 10-power magnification, but that normally aren't eye-visible.

I$_1$, I$_2$, & I$_3$: Imperfect—eye-visible flaws face up that range from just visible (I$_1$) to extremely visible to the naked eye (I$_3$). Some I$_2$ and I$_3$ diamonds may be damaged by ultrasonic cleaning. They may also be less resistant to knocks.

See Chapter 7 for photo examples of the various clarity grades.

| FL—IF | VVS | VS | SI | I$_1$ |

Diagram 1.1

CUTTING STYLE & STONE SHAPE: Some shapes such as rounds cost more than others like pear shapes. The effect of shape on price depends on the stone size, demand and available supply.

Brilliant-cut square diamonds (princess cuts) may cost slightly more than step-cut squares, depending on size. They have the same shape but different faceting styles.

Patented and trademarked cutting styles typically sell for more than generic cuts of the same shape.

The most dramatic impact of stone shape and cutting style on price is with fancy color diamonds because their face-up color can be intensified by the shape and faceting style, and because the rough is so expensive. The price difference between some shapes can range from 10% to 100% depending on the diamonds and the dealer selling the stone.

12

Fig. 1.8 What's wrong with the heart shaped diamond in this ring?

Answer: It looks cloudy instead of transparent. In this case, white reflections are making it look cloudy. The diamond is actually transparent. But some diamonds are inherently cloudy. If you want brilliance and sparkle, select a diamond with good transparency. Be fair to the diamond by making sure it's clean and well lighted when you examine it. *Photo by Wolf Pictures.*

TRANSPARENCY: Not all diamonds are transparent. Some are cloudy or translucent because they have finely divided particles which interrupt the passage of light. Normally, the higher the transparency the more valuable the diamond.

Even though transparency can have a significant impact on price, lab documents do not include it as a price factor. Gem labs, however, may take it into consideration when assigning a clarity grade. Some labs identify translucent diamonds as "fancy white diamonds" and may omit a clarity grade. This terminology does not change their inherent low value.

If you're interested in buying a brilliant diamond, choose one with high transparency. You don't need a lab report to help you do this. Your eye is the best judge of transparency. Make sure the diamonds you're comparing are clean, and be aware that transparency is an important price and beauty factor. For more information on evaluating transparency, see Chapter 7.

TREATMENT STATUS: Unlike colored gems, most diamonds are untreated. However, that is changing. Diamonds may undergo the following treatments to improve their clarity, color, transparency, and marketability: **fracture filling, laser drilling, irradiation, heating with high temperatures and high pressure,** and **coating.**

If you're buying an untreated diamond, have it identified as untreated on the receipt. Fracture filling, laser drilling and coatings can be detected by jewelers and appraisers. Accurate detection of irradiation and high temperature heat treatment normally requires the special expertise and sophisticated equipment of a qualified independent gem laboratory. An important reason for buying a diamond accompanied by a lab report is to verify that the diamond is untreated.

If a stone is identified as enhanced or processed, it's treated. Attractive untreated diamonds are still readily available. They will continue to be available if consumers ask for them.

What Kind of Diamond(s) Should You Buy?

If you were to ask ten jewelers this question, you'd probably get ten different answers. As in any other profession, there's disagreement as to what's best for consumers. This section gives my opinions and recommendations. There are other qualified people in the trade that may disagree with some of them.

You should base your choice of diamond(s) on the purpose for which it will be used. If you're buying a diamond for a wedding or engagement ring, it must be able to withstand a lifetime of daily wear and it should be worthy of being a symbol of eternal love. If you're buying diamonds for other jewelry such as stud earrings, durability and quality will be less important. If you're buying diamonds for resale or investment, the desires of potential buyers should influence your choices.

MY DIAMOND RECOMMENDATIONS FOR WEDDING & ENGAGEMENT RINGS:

Cut quality: A well-cut diamond should be a priority if you want your diamond to have good brilliance and sparkle. Chapter 6 will help you select a diamond that's well cut.

Color: It doesn't matter what color the diamond is as long as the person wearing it likes it. If you're looking for a traditional type of diamond without noticeable tints of yellow, buy one with a grade higher than L color. If you like warmer colors, consider buying color grades below K color. You'll be able to get a bigger and better diamond for the same amount of money as a colorless or near colorless diamond.

Because of their lower price, G and H colors are popular alternatives to D–F grades. Even people in the trade may have a hard time telling the difference between say an E- or G-color diamond when they're mounted in a ring.

If you have an ample budget and you'd like a distinctive diamond, consider getting one that's fancy color.

Carat weight: Any size is acceptable. Buy what you can afford.

Clarity: Avoid I_2 and I_3 clarity diamonds. They have inclusions that affect the beauty and/or threaten the durability of the stone. Consequently they're not as resistant to knocks as diamonds of higher clarity, nor are they as attractive. Some I_1 diamonds are acceptable for everyday wear, but generally your safest bet is to buy diamonds with a clarity of SI_2 or higher. A diamond doesn't need to be internally flawless or have a VVS grade to be beautiful. In fact as diamond treatments and synthetic diamonds become more prevalent, minor inclusions may become desirable features in diamonds because they can help prove that a stone is natural and untreated.

Cutting style & stone shape: Buy whatever you like best.

Transparency: Buy a transparent diamond(s). If a diamond is cloudy, it won't display adequate brilliance and sparkle no matter how well cut it is.

Treatment status: Buy untreated diamonds for reasons of durability and desirability. One of the main advantages of buying diamonds for bridal rings, instead of other gems is that natural diamonds are more resistant to abrasions and damage. They have withstood the test of time.

High temperature heat treatment has made some colored gemstones more brittle and susceptible to chipping and abrasions. We don't know yet what effect it has on the durability of diamonds. Likewise, you can't be certain if fracture-filled diamonds are resistant to knocks, a normal occurrence when they're mounted in everyday rings. Diamonds with large fractures, be they filled or unfilled, are not as durable as diamonds of good clarity.

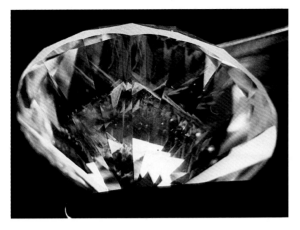

Fig. 1.9 The distinctive inclusion within this diamond gives it an imperfect clarity grade because it's so large and centrally located. However, since the inclusion is relatively clear, this 5-carat diamond looks better than some SI_2 stones when viewed face-up. It would make an attractive pendant, but it may not be the best choice for an everyday ring. Large inclusions can sometimes create strain, making a diamond more susceptible to damage from knocks against objects. Evaluate diamonds both with your eye and with a ten-power magnifier instead of relying solely on grades.

Untreated diamonds are more prized and much easier to sell than treated diamonds. They'll become more rare as diamond treatments increase. Why buy an enhanced diamond for something so special as a bridal ring when attractive, untreated diamonds are still readily available?

Since treated diamonds are harder to sell, they're disguised with euphemisms such as "clarity enhanced" and "processed," or else they're given an expensive sounding brand name. That's why it's important to ask if diamonds are treated or not. In addition, deal with sellers that will discuss and disclose treatments to you in clear language.

MY RECOMMENDATIONS FOR JEWELRY OTHER THAN BRIDAL RINGS

Cut quality: The diamonds should be cut well enough to display good brilliance and sparkle. Symmetry is not as important for diamonds in bracelets, brooches and necklaces as it is for the featured diamond of a bridal ring.

Color, carat weight, cutting style & shape: Same advice as for wedding and engagement rings.

Clarity: Avoid I_3 clarity diamonds. I_2 diamonds are acceptable if they have life and sparkle. In fact certain I_2 diamonds look better when mounted than some with a grade of I_1 or SI_3 (a grade seen on some lab reports, which is between I_1 and SI_2).

A piece featuring a high quality gemstone should be accented with diamonds of good quality.

Transparency: Buy jewelry with transparent diamonds. Two exceptions are jewelry pieces with black diamonds and pieces with patterns and designs requiring translucent white diamonds.

A lot of bargain-priced jewelry contains diamonds with inadequate transparency, which decreases their brilliance. When you're aware of this, it's easy to spot these diamonds in a showcase with your naked eye. Cloudy diamonds are not a good buy.

Treatment status: Treated diamonds can be an affordable option to buying natural diamonds. They can allow you to get a big look or unusual colors at a low price. If there's not a significant price difference between the enhanced or unenhanced stones, you're better off buying untreated diamonds. A few jewelers have charged customers a premium for heat and pressure treated diamonds. This is a real rip-off.

MY ADVICE ON DIAMONDS BOUGHT FOR POSSIBLE RESALE OR INVESTMENT

If you're not in the gem trade, you should buy a diamond to wear rather than to place in a safe deposit box. If you try to resell it to a dealer, they'll usually expect to buy it at less than wholesale. In addition, it's hard to find buyers when you're not in the diamond business. Nevertheless, it's normal for you to be interested in the resale potential of a diamond if you pay several thousand dollars for it. Here are some standards for investment diamonds.

Cut quality: Good symmetry as well as excellent brilliance are important. See Chapter 6 for guidelines on identifying top quality cuts. The standards for fancy color diamonds are more lenient because they're cut to maximize color.

Color: D–F color grades are customary for investment grade diamonds, but G–J colors are usually easier to sell because of their lower price. Fancy red, blue, pink and green diamonds can all be considered as an investment. Their high prices, however, limit the number of prospective buyers.

Carat weight: One carat or larger is the norm for investment diamonds, with the exception of rare fancy color diamonds, which may weigh less. Any size diamond is saleable.

Clarity: Flawless to VVS grades are typically recommended for investment grade diamonds. VS and SI grades, however, are often easier to sell because of their lower price. Flawless and internally flawless diamonds are best left in a safe deposit box. If they're mounted in a ring, they could get scratched and have their clarity grade and value lowered.

Clarity is not as important with fancy color diamonds. In fact, the diamond that holds the record for the highest per carat price ($926,000) had large, deep inclusions giving it an imperfect clarity. It was a 0.95 carat diamond with a fancy purplish red color.

Cutting style & shape: Round brilliant is the most saleable except in big sizes and fancy colors.

Transparency: High transparency is essential.

Treatment status: Buy only untreated diamonds if you plan to resell them.

Other Sources of Photos and Information on Diamonds

This chapter is just a brief summary of what you should look for when buying diamonds. To get a better understanding, read the rest of this book and examine the photos. Then cover up the captions and see if you can interpret the photos by yourself. Additional photo examples will be helpful. You'll find them in the following publications, which are all excellent references.

Collecting & Classifying Coloured Diamonds by Stephen Hofer: Ashland Press, New York

Diamond Grading ABC by Verena Pagel-Theisen: Rubin & Son, New York & Antwerp

The MicroWorld of Diamonds by John Koivula: Gemworld International, Northbrook, IL

Photo Masters For Diamond Grading by Gary Roskin: Gemworld International, Northbrook, IL

You can find photos and information on the latest research about diamonds in:

Australian Gemmologist. Gemmological Association of Australia, Brisbane

Gems and Gemology. Gemological Institute of America, Carlsbad, CA

Journal of Gemmology. Gemmological Association and Gem Testing Laboratory of Great Britain, London

2

The Diamond—Just Another Rock?

A Message From the Spokesman for the Diamond Kingdom

We diamonds have a couple confessions to make. We are not natural beauties and we are not forever.

Yes, it's true. When people see us lying in a stream or in a pile of dirt, they usually think we're just another rock. We look so ordinary. The first person that picked us up never dreamed we could both serve him and dazzle him. As time passed by, his descendants learned that we could cut any kind of rock or metal, but nothing could cut us except another diamond, so naturally we got drafted as saws, knives and drills. Yes, diamonds were used as tools long before they were cut as jewels.

Fig 2.1 A natural rough diamond covered with matrix—"skin" (upper right) and an octahedral-shaped diamond crystal (lower left).

We're proud of the Taj Majal in India. Its intricate marble designs were cut by diamond tools. We're equally proud to see how indispensable we are to twentieth-century man. He uses us to drill for oil and gas, to mine ores, to fashion gemstones, to cut metal parts for cars, rockets and farm machinery. Dentists use us to drill teeth. Surgeons use us to cut bone and tissue.

When man discovered that we diamonds can drill and cut better than anything else, he only began to recognize our potential. Outer space and defense programs take advantage of our ability to resist radiation, temperature and chemical damage. The electronics industry relies on us because not only can we conduct heat as well as any metal, we are also good electrical insulators. Think of us the next time you use a phone, a computer, a refrigerator, a television or an electric light. Is it any wonder that companies like General Electric and Japan's Sumitomo Electric Industries have spent so much time and money learning to create diamonds? Yes, man-made diamonds are now a reality.

Most of you people are probably more familiar with our optical qualities—our transparency, brilliance and sparkle. These have not only earned us a reputation as the most important gemstone, they have also increased our practical value by making us useful for lenses, lasers and windows for outer space.

Maybe you think we're conceited for telling you how good we are. We're only trying to prove that we're not just another rock. Actually, we'd be the first to admit that we're only simple folk. Coal and pencil lead are our next of kin. All of us are nothing but carbon, and that's why you can't say that diamonds are forever. When you heat us in oxygen up to about 700° C (1292° Fahrenheit), we start turning to carbon dioxide or carbon monoxide.

We can understand, though, that someone who has a hard time making it past the age of 100 would think that a diamond that's a few million years old is forever; but to us, a few million years isn't much. Your scientists are finally beginning to realize that we existed long before your solar system did, now that they're studying us in meteorites.

Man also has a hard time imagining that something so simple and practical as a diamond can be transformed into a handsome work of art. Maybe that's why it took him so long to bring out our inner beauty. It's only been in the last few hundred years that he's cut tiny geometrical windows around us to reflect and let in light. Until about 1919, most of us looked a bit lackluster compared to the way we look today. Then the mathematician Marcel Tolkowsky published a complex formula for cutting us that made us more brilliant.

The Tolkowsky formula and other similar ones can only work well on diamonds that pass the jewel qualifying exam—an inspection so severe that about 60% of all diamonds fail. This exam is a nightmare for us. The results determine whether we will bask under someone's appreciative eye or slave away as, perhaps, a drill.

After we've qualified as potential jewels, we undergo a beauty makeover that transforms us from ordinary looking rocks into extraordinary looking jewels. Makeover artists, also called diamond cutters, are in charge of this process. When they are finished, we start entering beauty contests. To get top scores in these contests, diamonds must have a lively and sparkling personality, an attractive shape, a clean character and individual charm. The judging is subjective and often there are hot debates over the scoring, particularly when large sums of prize money are at stake.

Fig. 2.2 The world's largest faceted diamond—the Golden Jubilee Diamond (545.67 carats). When it was found at South Africa's Premier Mine in 1986, it weighed 755.50 carats. Gabi Tolkowsky, a descendent of Marcel Tolkowsky, was commissioned to supervise the cutting of the stone. It took about two years to transform it into the beautiful golden (yellow-brown) diamond you see in this photograph. *Photo from the Asian Institute of Gemological Sciences (AIGS Thailand).*

You might expect that the winners of these beauty contests have the best lives. More often than not they end up stuck in a safe deposit box, especially the large diamonds. It's true that life as a drill is a real bore, but life in a dark lonely box is not much better. Occasionally, some of the winners end up in museums and have a pretty good life, but those diamonds that end up the happiest are those worn day in and day out by you. Yet these are not normally the diamonds with the highest scores.

I suspect you find it strange that I talk about diamonds being happy. Plato and other great philosophers knew that we diamonds are living beings and have the same types of feelings as humans, but for some reason, most of you don't want to accept this fact. Let me assure you that we diamonds do have feelings, both positive and negative.

We are angered and hurt when people are duped into losing their life savings on us, when workers in the diamond industry are exploited, when arguments, robberies, murders and wars occur because of us. Somebody even told us that we were part of the cause of the French revolution. It had something to do with a diamond necklace scandal. But, on second thought, maybe our role in that scandal was more positive than negative. When terrible things happen because of us, blame yourselves for misusing diamonds, don't blame us.

Fig. 2.3 Industrial rough diamond cubes set in jewelry by Todd Reed. *Photo by Azad.*

Fortunately life is not all bad; we do a lot of good. We create jobs for hundreds of thousands of people. We give people a means of escaping from oppressive governments. Non-jewel diamonds help supply you with food, energy, transportation, medical equipment and comfortable homes.

All of this good gives us great satisfaction, but there is something that gives us even more pleasure. It's when our mere presence makes man happy. What a joy it is to see the delight in the eye of newlyweds admiring their diamond wedding rings. What a joy it is to see a widow's grief interrupted by memories of some of the happiest moments of her life, as she looks down at her diamond engagement ring. What a joy it is to see people momentarily forget their everyday worries and frustrations and focus on thoughts of beauty and love, as they glance at us on their hands or wrists.

As long as you enjoy us and use us toward good ends, we diamonds don't expect anything in return for brightening up your lives. Well, maybe that's a bit of a lie. We will be bold enough to ask one little favor of you. Its this: If anyone ever tries to tell you that the diamond is just another rock, please tell him he's full of poppycock.

3

Carat Weight

Which sounds more impressive?

♦ *One-carat diamond*

♦ *Diamond weighing one-fifth of a gram*

♦ *200-milligram diamond*

All three diamonds are the same weight. So if you thought *one-carat diamond* sounds more impressive, then you can understand why the jewelry industry prefers to use *carats* instead of *grams* to express gemstone weight. The term *carat* originated in ancient times when gemstones were weighed against the carob bean. Each bean weighed about one carat. In 1913, carat weight was standardized internationally and adapted to the metric system.

The weight of small diamonds is frequently expressed in points, with one point equaling 0.01 carats. For example, five points is a short way of saying five one-hundredths of a carat. Diamonds weighing 0.05 ct are referred to as five pointers. Examine the following written and spoken forms of carat weight:

Table 3.1

Written	Spoken
0.005 ct (0.5 pt)	half point
0.05 ct	five points
0.25 ct	twenty-five points or quarter carat
0.50 ct	fifty points or half carat
1.82 cts	one point eight two (carats) or one eighty-two

Note that *point* when used in expressing weights over one carat refers to the decimal point, not a unit of measure. Also note that *pt* can be used instead of *ct* to make people think their diamond is 100 times heavier than it is.

Effect of Carat Weight on Price

Most people are familiar with the principle, the higher the carat weight the greater the diamond value. However, in actual practice, this principle is more complicated than it appears.

This can be illustrated by having you arrange the following four rings in the order of decreasing diamond value. Assume that the quality, shape and color of all the diamonds are the same.

  a. 1-carat diamond solitaire ring (one diamond only)
  b. 1-carat TW, 24-diamond wedding ring
  c. 2-carat diamond solitaire ring
  d. 2-carat TW, 48-diamond wedding ring

In almost all cases, the order of decreasing value would be $c > a > d > b$. In rare cases, the order might be $c > d > a > b$. Strangely enough, a single one-carat diamond usually costs more than two carats of small diamonds of the same quality. This is because the supply of larger diamonds is limited. So when you compare ring prices, you should pay attention to individual diamond weights and **notice the difference between** the labels **1 ct TW** (one carat total weight) and **1 ct** (the weight of one stone). A ring with a **1 ct**, colorless, top quality diamond can be worth more than 10 times as much as a ring with **1 ct TW** diamonds of the same quality.

When comparing diamond cost, you should also start noting the **per-carat cost** instead of concentrating on the stone cost or the total diamond cost. To understand why, try comparing the cost of the following three diamonds. Assume they're the same color, shape and quality.

Weight	Total Stone Cost
1.00 ct	$6,000
1.20 ct	$7,080
1.30 ct	$7,540

Most people would find it hard to determine the best value just by looking at the total stone cost. Now try to compare values by looking at the per-carat cost of the same diamonds.

Weight	Per-Carat Cost
1.00 ct	$6.000
1.20 ct	$5,900
1.30 ct	$5,800

Normally, the 1.30 ct diamond should cost the same or more per-carat than the other two stones. However, in this case, it costs less. Consequently, the 1.30 ct stone is the best buy. But it's only when we compare the per-carat prices of the stones that this becomes evident. Therefore **when you shop for diamonds, think in terms of the per-carat cost.** This is what diamond dealers do. To calculate the per-carat cost or the total cost of a diamond, use the following equations:

$$\textbf{Per-carat cost} = \frac{\textbf{stone cost}}{\textbf{carat weight}}$$

Total cost of a stone = carat weight x per-carat cost

Diamonds can be divided into weight categories. These categories often vary from one dealer to another but may be outlined as follows:

Table 3.2 Weight Categories for Diamonds		
0.01 – 0.03 ct	0.30 – 0.37 ct	0.96 – 0.99 ct
0.04 – 0.07 ct	0.38 – 0.45 ct	1.00 – 1.49 ct
0.08 – 0.14 ct	0.46 – 0.49 ct	1.50 – 1.99 ct
0.15 – 0.17 ct	0.50 – 0.69 ct	2.00 – 2.49 ct
0.18 – 0.22 ct	0.70 – 0.89 ct	2.50 – 2.99 ct
0.23 – 0.29 ct	0.90 – 0.95 ct	3.00 – 3.99 ct

The above weight categories are based mainly on those listed in the *Rapaport Diamond Report*. As diamonds move up from one weight category to another, their prices may increase from about 5% to 50%. So if you buy, for example, a 0.97 ct diamond instead of a 1 carat, you'll normally pay less per carat, even though the stone will resemble a one-carat diamond. Low-quality diamonds tend to show less of a price differential between categories than those of high quality.

There are a couple exceptions to the rule that as diamond weight increases, per-carat value increases. Because of high demand, diamonds weighing 5, 10 or 15 points may cost more per carat than larger odd-size diamonds. Also, better quality .01 ct- to .035-ct diamonds have sometimes cost more per carat than diamonds weighing from .06 ct to .08 ct. This was the case during 1987-89, when there was an unusually high demand for three pointers for tennis bracelets.

The complexity of diamond pricing can be discouraging, but you don't need to know the details of the system to shop for value. Just be aware that carat weight as well as other factors can affect the per-carat value of diamonds and follow these two guidelines:

♦ Compare the per-carat cost instead of the total cost.

♦ When judging prices, compare diamonds of the same size, shape, quality and color.

Estimating Carat Weight

If you buy a diamond ring in a reputable jewelry store, you normally don't have to know how to estimate the carat weight of the diamonds because the weight will be marked on the ring. However, if you buy diamond jewelry at flea markets or auctions, it's to your advantage to know how to roughly estimate weight.

Probably the easiest way to estimate weight is to carry a diamond weight estimator with you. It's an inexpensive piece of metal or plastic that has cutouts or diagrams of diamond sizes corresponding to various diamond weights. They can be found in jewelry supply stores. You can also estimate weight by referring to Table 3.3. It shows the corresponding sizes of round-brilliant diamonds of various weights. Weight estimators and charts which do not take into consideration the depth of a diamond or its girdle thickness can only give a general idea of the weight. (The girdle is the rim around the diamond. See Chapter 4 for a diagram of diamond parts.)

Weight can also be estimated by measuring the stone with a gauge and calculating its weight with formulas such as those in Table 3.4.

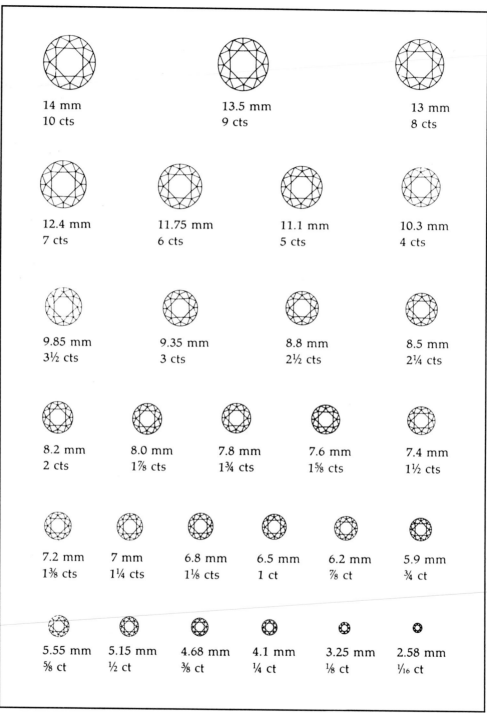

14 mm
10 cts

13.5 mm
9 cts

13 mm
8 cts

12.4 mm
7 cts

11.75 mm
6 cts

11.1 mm
5 cts

10.3 mm
4 cts

9.85 mm
3½ cts

9.35 mm
3 cts

8.8 mm
2½ cts

8.5 mm
2¼ cts

8.2 mm
2 cts

8.0 mm
1⅞ cts

7.8 mm
1¾ cts

7.6 mm
1⅝ cts

7.4 mm
1½ cts

7.2 mm
1⅜ cts

7 mm
1¼ cts

6.8 mm
1⅛ cts

6.5 mm
1 ct

6.2 mm
⅞ ct

5.9 mm
¾ ct

5.55 mm
⅝ ct

5.15 mm
½ ct

4.68 mm
⅜ ct

4.1 mm
¼ ct

3.25 mm
⅛ ct

2.58 mm
1/16 ct

Table 3.3 Diameters and corresponding weights of round, brilliant-cut diamonds. *Diagram courtesy of the GIA (Gemological Institute of America).*

Table 3.4 Diamond Weight Estimation Formulas*	
Round Brilliant	Average diameter^2 x depth x .0061
Oval Brilliant	Average diameter^2 x depth x .0062 (avg. diameter = L + W ÷ 2)
Heart-Shape Brilliant	Length x width x depth x .0059
Square Brilliant	Length x width x depth x .0085
Triangular Brilliant	Length x width x depth x .0057
Pear Shape	Length x width x depth x .00615 if length/width ratio is 1.25:1 Length x width x depth x .00600 if length/width ratio is 1.50:1 Length x width x depth x .00575 if length/width ratio is 2.00:1
Marquise	Length x width x depth x .00565 if length/width ratio is 1.50:1 Length x width x depth x .00580 if length/width ratio is 2.00:1 Length x width x depth x .00585 if length/width ratio is 2.50:1
Emerald Cut	Length x width x depth x .0080 if length/width ratio is 1.00:1 Length x width x depth x .0092 if length/width ratio is 1.50:1 Length x width x depth x .0100 if length/width ratio is 2.00:1

* These formulas were developed for stones with good proportions. Add 2% for slightly thick girdles and from 4% to 10% for thick to extremely thick girdles. Keep in mind that the only accurate means of determining the weight of a stone is to take it out of its setting and weigh it. This, however, is not always possible nor advisable. The source of these formulas is mainly the *GIA Diamond Grading Laboratory Manual*.

Size Versus Carat Weight

Sometimes in the jewelry trade, the term "size" is used as a synonym for "carat weight." This is because small round diamonds having the same weight also look the same size and have similar diameters. As diamonds increase in weight, their size becomes less predictable. This means that a 0.90-carat round diamond can look bigger than a 1.00-carat round diamond, especially if the lighter-weight stone is cut shallow. So if size is important to you, consider diamond measurements as well as carat weight. You don't need to carry a millimeter gauge when you go shopping. Just start noting the different illusions of size that different diamond measurements can create. Chapter 6 explains how diamond proportions affect size and beauty. Diamonds that look big for their weight may have reduced brilliance and fire.

You should also note that diamonds usually have different measurements than other gemstones having the same weight. For example, because of its high density, a one-carat cubic zirconia is considerably smaller than a one-carat diamond. On the other hand, a one-carat emerald, due to its lower density, is bigger than a one-carat diamond. We can compare gem sizes by comparing their **specific gravity** (the ratio of a gem's weight to the weight of an equal volume of water at 4$^{°C}$). The specific gravity of diamond is 3.52 ($\pm$.01) whereas that of cubic zirconia is 5.80 ($\pm$.20) and that of emerald is 2.72 (+.18, -.05).

In Chapter 4, you'll learn about a variety of diamond shapes and cutting styles. These, too, can play an important role in determining the apparent size of a stone.

Fig. 4.1 The Gabrielle® diamond—a new style of brilliant cut, which is available in a variety of shapes—(clockwise from top left) round, octagonal rectangle, pear shape, oval, marquise, octagonal square, and heart. The Gabrielle® has 105 facets and was named after its creator, the renowned master diamond cutter, Gabriel (Gabi) Tolkowsky. *Photo from Suberi Bros.*

4

Shape & Cutting Style

The shape of a diamond not only affects how big and brilliant it looks, but it may even reveal personality traits of the buyer.

Saul Spero, a New York diamond appraiser and gem consultant, spent twenty-five years interviewing over 50,000 people and developing a system of predicting personality types mainly based on a person's first three preferences of diamond shapes. In his book *Diamonds, Love & Compatibility*, Spero discusses the six basic shapes—round, oval, pear, heart, marquise and square or rectangle. He states that if a woman has an exclusive preference for any of these shaped diamonds, she could be characterized as follows:

Exclusive preference for	Personality Type
Round	Home- and family-centered, dependable, unaggressive, easy to get along with and security conscious.
Oval	Individualistic, creative, well-organized, dependable, willing to take chances
Heart	Sentimental, creative, feminine, sensitive, trusting, dramatic and a dreamer
Rectangle / Square	Disciplined, organized, conservative, efficient, honest and open
Pear	Conforming, considerate, adaptable, home-and community-centered
Marquise	Extroverted, aggressive, experimental, exciting, innovative, career-centered

Please note that the personality profiles above are for women who like only one shape. Most women like more than one diamond shape, which is why Spero also evaluated personality types in terms of their second and third choices. A more complete discussion on diamond shape and personality can be found in Spero's book.

There are more than the six preceding shapes to choose from. Triangular shapes are very popular. You can also find stars, animals, Christmas trees, fish, fruit, boats and letters of the alphabet (figs 4.2 and 4.3). Some people even have diamonds cut in the form of their state, province or country. Stones with unusual shapes are sometimes called **fantasy cuts**.

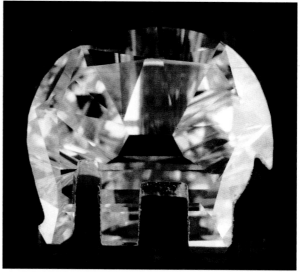

Fig. 4.2 A fantasy cut that's trademarked "Sculptaire." *Photo from Global Diamonds.*

Fig. 4.3 Another fantasy cut

Diamond Terms Defined

Before you can thoroughly understand a discussion of diamond shapes and styles, some terminology must be explained. Here are some basic terms:

Facets	The flat, polished surfaces or planes on a diamond.
Table	The large, flat, top facet. It has an octagonal shape on a round brilliant diamond.
Bezel Facets	Kite-shape facets on the crown of brilliant-cut diamonds. The star, pavilion mains, and upper and lower girdle facets are other facets found on brilliant cuts (fig. 4.4).
Culet	The tiny facet on the pointed bottom of the pavilion, parallel to the table.
Girdle	The narrow rim around the diamond. The girdle plane is parallel to the table and is the largest diameter of any part of the stone.
Crown	The upper part of the diamond above the girdle.
Pavilion	The lower part of the diamond below the girdle. It's cone-shaped on a round diamond.
Brilliant Cut	The most common style of diamond cutting. The standard brilliant cut consists of 32 facets plus a table above the girdle and 24 facets plus a culet below the girdle (fig. 4.4). Other shapes besides round can be faceted as brilliant cuts.
Fancy Shape	Any shape except round. A pear shape is an example of a fancy shape. Sometimes fancy shapes are simply called **fancies**.

28

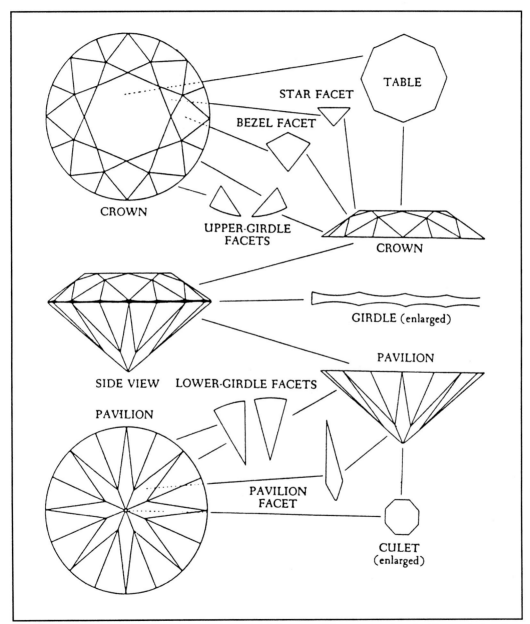

Fig. 4.4 Facet arrangement of a standard round brilliant cut. *Diagram reprinted with permission from the Gemological Institute of America.*

Fig. 4.5 Step-cut tapered baguette

Cutting Styles

The two concepts of shape and cutting style are often described by one term in the jewelry trade. For example, when a jeweler uses the term **baguette**, he's referring to a square-cornered, rectangular-shaped diamond with rows of step-like facets (fig. 4.6). If the two long sides of the baguette taper inward, it's called a **tapered baguette** (figs. 4.5 & 4.8).

The GIA has simplified the description of diamond cutting styles by limiting them to three basic types—step cut, brilliant cut and mixed cut. These are described below:

Step Cut Has rows of facets which are usually four-sided and elongated and parallel to the girdle. Examples include the baguette (fig 4.6) and tapered baguettes (figs. 4.5 & 4.8). If step-cuts have clipped-off corners, they're called **emerald cuts** because emeralds are often cut this way (figs. 4.7 & 4.9). This protects the corners and provides places where prongs can secure the stone. Emerald cuts are in essence step-cut, octagonal rectangles. They tend to have more facets than baguettes. Emerald-cut diamonds are usually rectangular or square, but they can also be triangular (fig. 4.10).

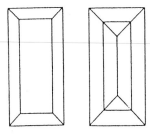

Fig. 4.6 Step-cut baguette

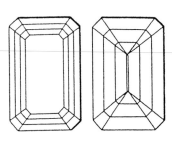

Fig. 4.7 Emerald cut

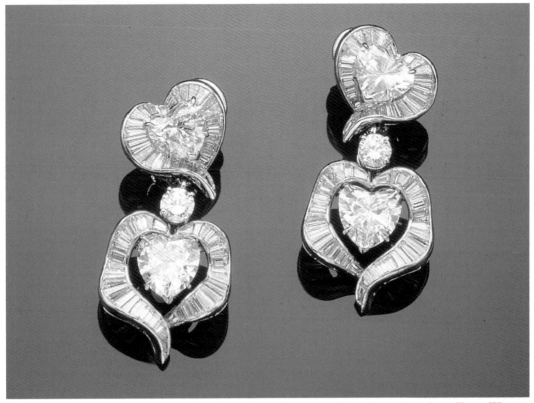

Fig. 4.8 Tapered baguettes surrounding heart-shape diamonds. *Photo & earrings from Harry Winston.*

Fig. 4.9 Emerald-cut diamond ring (20.14 cts). *Photo and ring from Harry Winston, Inc.*

Fig. 4.10 Emerald-cut (step-cut) triangle

Fig. 4.11 Old mine cut, face-up view.

Fig. 4.12 Side view of diamond in fig 4.14

Brilliant cut

Has triangular-, kite-, or lozenge-shaped facets that radiate outward around the stone. Diagram 4.14 is an example of a heart-shaped brilliant cut with 58 facets. Four other modifications of the brilliant-cut style are the single cut, rose cut, old mine cut and the old European cut. The **single cut**, which has 17 or 18 facets, is used on very small diamonds (fig. 4.13 & 4.15). The jewelry trade generally refers to round diamonds with 18 facets as **single cuts** and to those with 58 facets as **full cuts** or traditional **round brilliants**.

Fig. 4.13 Single cut

In some antique jewelry and even some contemporary jewelry, you may see the **rose cut** (fig. 4.16). It has triangular brilliant-style facets, a pointed dome-shaped crown, a flat base and a circular girdle outline. The rose cut, which probably originated in India, was introduced into Europe by Venetian polishers in the fifteenth century.

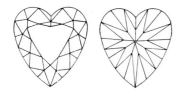
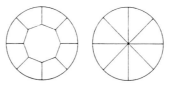

Fig. 4.14 Heart shaped brilliant cut   **Fig. 4.15** Single cut   **Fig. 4.16** Rose cut

The **old mine** and **old European cuts** typically have 58 facets, a high crown, a small table and a large culet. Old mine cuts are **cushion shaped** (squarish with rounded corners and sides), whereas old European cuts are round. These older cuts were fashioned before the early 1900's when diamond saws were invented. Consequently, their proportions resemble the original rough, with the crown height similar to the pavilion depth. The modern round brilliant is cut with a lower crown, which displays more brilliance.

Gemstone pendants or earrings are occasionally cut as **briolettes** (fig. 4.17). These have a tear-drop shape, a circular cross-section and brilliant-style facets (or occasionally rectangular, step-cut style facets).

32

Fig. 4.17 Diamond necklace with a 32-carat briolette pendant. *Photo & necklace from Harry Winston, Inc.*

Fig. 4.18 Old European cut

Fig. 4.19 Old European-cut diamonds set in earrings. *Photo and earrings from Ebert & Company.*

Mixed Cut   Has both step- and brilliant-cut facets. The pavilion, for example, can be step cut and the crown can be brilliant cut, but the step- and brilliant-cut facets can also be scattered over the diamond. This cut is used a lot more on transparent colored stones than on diamonds.

Fig. 4.20 Oval mixed cut

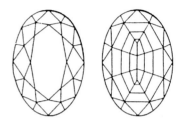

Fig. 4.21 Oval mixed cut diagram

When you shop for diamonds, you may hear salespeople talk about Radiants, trilliants and Quadrillions—styles which have been introduced within about the last twenty-five years. To better understand what they're talking about, you can refer to the following descriptions and photos:

Radiant   A brilliant-cut square or rectangle with clipped-off corners like the emerald cut. It has 70 facets. The Radiant (fig. 4.23) was designed and patented by Henry Grossbard of New York and is marketed by the I. Starck Co., Inc. of Chicago. It was first introduced in 1976 in Hong Kong.

Trilliant   The name used by the Royal Asscher Diamond Company of Amsterdam for a triangular brilliant cut with curved sides and a high crown. Today "trilliant" is used as a general term for any brilliant-cut triangle (fig. 4.24).

Trielle   The trademarked name for a triangular brilliant designed by the Trillion Diamond Co., a subsidiary of LF Industries. The trielle was developed in the 1950's by Leon Finker and patented in 1978 under the name of LF Industries in New York. Prior to 1991, the patented brand name for the Trielle was the **Trillion**. Now the term "trillion" is used to refer to any brilliant-cut triangle.

Quadrillion   A square diamond with 49 brilliant-style facets—21 crown facets, 24 pavilion facets and four girdle facets. The Quadrillion is designed to maximize brilliancy and minimize undesirable light leakage in square diamonds. It was patented and trademarked by Ambar Diamonds of Los Angeles in 1981. Figure 4.22 features a 2.05-ct Quadrillion accented by several smaller Quadrillions.

Princess Cut   A brilliant-cut square, rectangle or cushion shape, which may have from 57 to 70 facets and variable proportions (fig. 4.25 & 4.26). Like the Quadrillion, its pavilion facets widen towards the culet and narrow towards the corners to form a pattern resembling a four-pointed star.

Fig. 4.22 The Quadrillions in this 18K gold ring give it a very brilliant look. *Photo and ring from Ambar Diamonds.*

Fig. 4.23 Radiant

Fig. 4.24 Trilliant

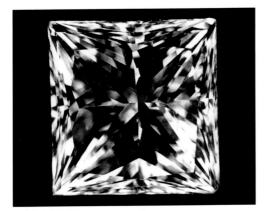

Fig. 4.25 Princess cut, face up

Fig. 4.26 Princess cut, pavilion side up

Fig. 4.27 The Zoë®, a completely new cutting style. *Photo from Suberi Bros.*

The **Zoë® Diamond**, was unveiled in the year 2000 to mark the next 100 years as a symbol of beauty and emotion. It has 100 symmetrical facets on the crown and pavilion and 96 on the girdle. The table facet is surrounded by nine facets.

Gabi Tolkowsky, the creator of the Zoë®, won world-wide acclaim in the late 80's for designing, cutting and polishing the Centenary Diamond, the largest colorless, flawless modern-cut diamond (273.85 cts). Gabi also cut and polished the "Golden Jubilee," a 545.67 ct golden colored diamond which was a gift to the King of Thailand. It holds the record for being the world's largest polished diamond.

Distributed exclusively by Suberi Bros., the Zoë® was designed to create an eternal motion of images and light within the diamond that gives you shivers up your spine as you view it.

New Cutting Styles

New styles for cutting diamonds are continuously being developed. One new brilliant-cut style is the Gabrielle®, shown in figure 4.1 on page 26, which has 105 facets. The Zoë® Diamond with its 100 facets is another patented style (fig. 4.27).

Baguettes, which are traditionally step cut, are now being made with brilliant style facets to add more brilliance. One patented brilliant-cut baguette is the Bagillion™. Another unique style for rectangular diamonds is the Crisscut™, which has 77 crisscrossed facets designed to increase brilliance (figs. 4.28 & 4.29). It was patented in 1998.

Fig. 4.28 A Crisscut™ diamond by Christopher Designs. *Photography by Christony Inc.*

Fig. 4.29 Crisscut™ diamonds in a ring created by Christopher Designs. *Photo by Christony Inc.*

If you're looking for a diamond with an ultramodern look, you might want to consider the Spirit Sun®, also called the "Spirit Diamond." It has 32 facets with 16 triangular facets that radiate on both the crown and the pavilion, creating a bright and reflective face. It was developed by Dr. Ulrich Freiesleben of Münster, Germany in collaboration with Bernd Munsteiner. Because of its larger facets, the Spirit Sun® is ideal for displaying the color of fancy-color diamonds. Dr. Freiesleben's goal when creating the Spirit Sun® was to honor the essence of the diamond by aiming for simplicity, clarity and optimal light reflection.

Fig. 4.30 The Spirit Sun®

The Effect of Shape & Cutting Style on Diamond Prices

The shape of a diamond can play an important role in determining its price. For example:

♦ A 0.07-carat square may cost up to 20% more than a round diamond of the same weight, color, and quality.

♦ A 1-carat colorless round diamond might cost 15%–30% more than a one-carat square diamond of the same color grade and quality.

♦ A 1-carat, intense-yellow round diamond can cost from 10% to over 100% more than a radiant with the same weight and color grade, depending on the stones and the dealer selling them.

There are a variety of reasons why round and fancy-shape diamonds are priced differently. Small rounds are sometimes priced lower than fancy shapes because of lower inventory and labor costs. (The additional labor cost of small fancies is partially due to the specialized skills needed to cut them). Small rounds sell more quickly so less of a profit margin is needed to cover the cost of keeping them in inventory. It's less time consuming to cut, measure, and select small rounds than small fancy shapes. Consequently, labor costs can be lower. However, the price differential between small round and fancy-shape diamonds sometimes decreases to the point where both are priced about the same during periods of very high demand for small rounds.

In sizes over one-fourth carat, rounds usually cost more than other shapes. The percentage difference can vary, though, depending on the size and quality of the stone, the supply and demand at the time of sale, and the dealer selling the stones. Since the pricing of the different shapes is complex, it's easiest for consumers to simply compare stones of the same shape when pricing diamonds.

Inventory costs for large rounds can be just as high as those for large fancy shapes because there are fewer buyers in the market for larger, more expensive diamonds. In addition, there is a greater demand for round diamonds than for fancies, so large round diamonds tend to cost more than most fancy shapes of the same size and quality.

Fancy shapes may display a stronger face-up color than rounds cut from the same rough. This is one of the main reasons intense yellow round diamonds cost more than intense yellow radiants. The rough of the round diamond must be darker than that of the radiant to achieve the

same intense yellow face-up color, partly because cutters can't play as much with the angles and shape of rounds to maximize the color. The stronger the color of the rough, the higher the price of the rough. The final price of the diamond is based to a large degree on the cost of the rough.

The shape of a rough diamond crystal before it's cut also plays a role in diamond pricing. When long diamond crystals are cut into ovals, pears and emerald cuts, they normally weigh more than if they had been cut into rounds. This means the per carat cost of the fancy shape can be lower than a round and still bring the same amount of profit from the original rough diamond.

Cutting style can have a slight effect on prices. Radiants (octagonal brilliant cuts) may cost slightly more or less than emerald cuts (octagonal step cuts) of the same size, color and quality depending on what is currently in demand. Trademarked cutting styles usually cost more than generic cuts. Sometimes the price difference is due to the quality of the cutting.

Judging Shape

Diamond prices are not only affected by the shape type (i.e. pear, marquise, round, etc.), they're also affected by the attractiveness of the chosen shape. For example, an unsymmetrical or a long and skinny marquise diamond can't command the same price as a well-shaped marquise.

The following diagrams show desirable shape outlines of five basic shapes. A knowledge of the ideal round shape is assumed.

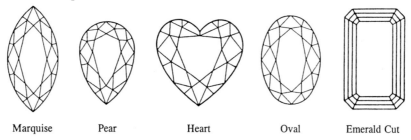

| Marquise | Pear | Heart | Oval | Emerald Cut |

Fig. 4.31 *Diagrams courtesy of the Gemological Institute of America*

Let's look at some diamonds with shape outlines that do not conform to industry standards.

Fig. 4.32 If you cut the diamond in this figure in half, the shape of the two parts would not be equal. Even though many people like free forms, symmetrical stones usually are more valued.

Fig 4.33 Note the width of this pear shape. There is nothing intrinsically wrong with this stone. In fact, it could flatter a long, slender hand. The jewelry industry, however, places a greater value on a pear with a more traditional shape.

Fig. 4.34 This diamond is long and skinny. Even though it is priced less than a more traditional pear-shape stone, it could be very flattering on someone with a broad hand.

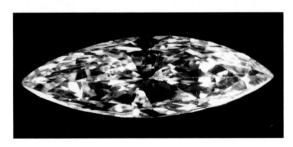

Fig. 4.35 A long, skinny marquise

Fig. 4.36 This diamond looks more like a shield than a pear-shape. Some people prefer this shape, so this is best for them. But normally, stones having another shape than intended should cost a little less.

If you're buying a diamond for your own personal pleasure, its shape doesn't matter, as long as you like it. However, if you're buying your diamond mainly as an investment, you'd be wise to select a shape conforming to industry ideals. Such shapes are often sold at premium prices and might be hard to find.

You may be wondering why all diamonds are not cut to industry standards since they would be worth more. It's because too much of the original diamond rough would be lost if it were always cut away to form standard diamond shapes. So if the diamond rough is elongated, one can expect the cutter to fashion an elongated diamond. Buyers have different tastes, too, and many of them prefer non-traditional shapes, particularly if they can buy them at a lower price per carat.

What Shape Diamond is Best for You?

To answer this question, let's consider some of the factors that will determine what shape diamond is best for you.

♦ **Your personal preference.** This should play the greatest role in your choice. There's no point in wearing a diamond if you don't like its looks. However, most people like more than one shape. Therefore, it's helpful for them to know how the various shapes affect a diamond's brilliance, apparent size and price.

♦ **The amount of brilliance and sparkle you want your diamond to display.** The shape and cutting style that shows the most brilliance and sparkle is a brilliant-cut round. This is probably the biggest reason why round diamonds under three carats are more popular than other shapes.
Emerald cuts have less sparkle than brilliant cuts, but many people like their sleek, elegant look. People who would prefer a rectangular or square diamond with more sparkle can buy a Quadrillion, Radiant, Crisscut or princess cut.
Although fancy shapes aren't normally as brilliant as rounds, when they're cut properly, they can display a great deal of brilliance. There are more factors than just shape and cutting style which influence the brilliance of a diamond. Chapter 6 will explain these in more detail.

♦ **How much you want your diamond to weigh.** In sizes over three carats, fancy-shape diamonds often outsell round diamonds. This is because many people think that large, fancy-shape diamonds look more elegant and less pretentious than large round ones. If you're buying a big diamond, see how the various shaped diamonds look on your hand. Then make your choice.

♦ **How big you want your diamond to look.** A lot of people want their diamond to look as big as possible, even if it doesn't weigh much. Fancy shapes generally look bigger than round diamonds of equal weight, particularly if they're elongated like the marquise and pear. The Trielle is also known for looking bigger than it weighs. The people that market it claim that it looks nearly 50% larger than a round brilliant diamond of the same weight because it's cut wide and shallow.

♦ **The shape and size of your hand.** The shape of your diamond can give the illusion that your hand looks longer or shorter than it is. For example, a long, thin diamond set lengthwise along your finger can make your hand look longer and thinner. A broad diamond or long one set horizontally across your finger can make your hand look broader and shorter. Try on a few shapes and see which one flatters your hand the most.

Fig. 4.37 The sparkle of the brilliant-cut marquises, pears and rounds contrasted with the sleek beauty of the two emerald cuts creates a striking pair of diamond earrings. One of the emerald-cuts is 24.04 cts and the other, 20.14 carats. *Photo and earrings from Harry Winston, Inc.*

♦ **The color and clarity of the diamond.** The shape and cutting style that can best mask flaws and yellow tints is the round brilliant. In emerald cuts and baguettes, the flaws become the most obvious. What this means is that a low quality, less expensive, round brilliant can look very good to the naked eye, whereas a step-cut rectangular or triangular diamond of the same quality might look unacceptable.

♦ **The availability of the shapes.** Even if you like a specific shape, you may find that there is a poor selection in the size or quality you want to buy. For example, you might have a hard time finding a well-shaped one-carat marquise and end up buying another shape instead. If you have your heart set on a specific shape, ask your jeweler to find it for you. He can call around to various diamond dealers until he finds the diamond that meets your needs, but be prepared to give him the time he needs to find your stone.

♦ **Your purpose for buying the diamond—pleasure or investment**. If you're buying a diamond for personal pleasure, any shape you like can be a good choice. But if resale for profit is your goal, you need to consider what shapes are most in demand and are likely to stay in demand. If the diamond is less than three carats in weight, you are more likely to find a buyer for a round diamond. For stones over three carats, you will probably find it hard to find an immediate buyer no matter what shape you buy, mainly because so few people can afford investment quality diamonds that size. However, fancy shapes might be a better choice for stones over three carats since they tend to outsell large round diamonds.

To simplify this discussion on choosing a diamond shape, we've only considered diamond solitaires. There are other factors to consider when selecting cocktail rings, anniversary bands or any ring with many small diamonds. Round diamonds are the most popular for these rings, partly because rounds are easier to set, match, and replace. In addition, small rounds are often less expensive than small fancy shapes. However, fancy shapes permit distinctive styles. You should therefore be aware that rings with small fancies usually cost more and require more labor than those with small round brilliants. This will help you realize the importance of comparing rings having diamonds of the same shape as well as the same size, color and clarity. Then, you'll be able to judge value more accurately.

Fig. 5.1 This delicate peacock feather pin features an 8-carat, natural-color green diamond together with pink, yellow and near colorless diamonds. Sapphires and emeralds encircle the pink diamonds. *Photo and pin from Harry Winston, Inc.*

Fig. 5.2 Blue and colorless diamond earrings with two interchangeable drops—a 7.08 carat blue diamond and a 7.38 carat F-color diamond. *Photo and earrings from Harry Winston, Inc.*

5

Diamond Color

W hen you look at diamonds in jewelry stores, they may all seem colorless. But if you look closely, you'll notice that they normally have slight tints of yellow, gray or brown. The strength of these tints partially determines the price of the diamond. Normally the less color a diamond has the more it costs. However, prices start rising when the color reaches a point just stronger than light yellow (a grade designated as **fancy yellow**). As the intensity of fancy-yellow diamonds increases so does their price. Four-carat diamonds with a very intense yellow color have commanded prices as high as $50,000 per carat.

The most widely used color grading system is the one developed by the GIA (Gemological Institute of America), which identifies colors with alphabetical letters ranging from D to Z+. It is so well known throughout the world that even if your jeweler uses another system, he should know how to translate his grades into GIA grades. The following diagram helps explain the meaning of the GIA color grades. Brown and gray diamonds are graded on the same scale.

D E F*	G H I J	K L M	N to Z	Z+
colorless	near colorless	faint yellow	very light to light yellow	fancy yellow

(*Colorless for 0.50 ct or less, near colorless for heavier stones)

In terms of price, D (no color) is the most expensive color and N through Z (the darker colors) the least expensive. D, E and F represent the most expensive diamond color grades because they are rare and in high demand. The nuances of color are so fine between the grades that the average consumer cannot tell the difference between a D and F color. However, the price difference between D and F color diamonds may be as much as a 10% to 20%, depending on their size and clarity. Professionals must rely on comparison stones to determine color grades, and even then it can be hard to distinguish between a D or E color diamond, for example.

If you're interested in a diamond that looks colorless, stones with a grade from D to J can meet your needs. When they're mounted, it's not easy to see the difference between colorless and near colorless grades face up. If you prefer warmer colors, consider getting a color above K. It's better to compromise on color than on cut quality and transparency when your budget is limited. D to J color diamonds are sometimes referred to as **white diamonds**. This book normally uses the term colorless to describe these diamonds because "white" is not an accurate color description. In addition, there are translucent milky diamonds which are really white, making the term "white diamond" an ambiguous term. You should know, however, that if a trade professional describes one diamond as whiter than others, this normally means the stone has a higher color grade.

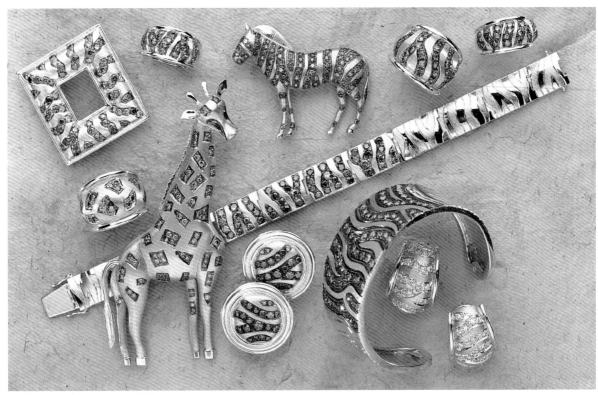

Fig. 5.3 Brown diamonds creatively used in 18K gold jewelry. *Photo & jewelry from Timeless Gem Designs.*

Fig. 5.4 An attractive brown diamond accented by colorless baguettes. *The photo and ring are from Extrême Gioielli.*

Fig. 5.5 Platinum rings set with brown and colorless Gabrielle diamonds. The rings are also available with pink or yellow diamonds. *Photo from Suberi Bros.*

If you're buying the diamond for personal enjoyment, it doesn't matter what color you select as long as you like it and it looks good on you. But if you're buying the diamond for investment purposes, you're better off selecting an untreated diamond in the D to F range.

Diamonds with a tinge of yellow (K to Z grades) are fairly common. Consequently, they are less expensive than colorless diamonds and often used in discount jewelry. This doesn't signify they're inferior. Some people prefer a yellow tint because it conveys a feeling of warmth or because it might look good with their skin color. Fine quality jewelry stores also use these diamonds in their jewelry in order to meet the needs of all their clientele.

In order to see the difference between colorless and faint yellow diamonds when they're mounted in jewelry, you'll probably have to put jewelry pieces with the two qualities side by side. The yellowish diamonds will blend in more with the gold and the colorless diamonds will provide more of a contrast and probably look brighter. The color difference is more obvious when you view loose diamonds through the side with the table (top facet) down as in figure 5.6.

Not all diamonds in the K to Z range are yellowish. Some are brownish. Brownish tinted diamonds are the least expensive color of diamonds used for jewelry because there's less of a market for them. If diamond rings are being promoted at unusually low prices, there's a good chance that brownish goods have been used. This doesn't mean these rings are of inferior quality. It only means that the store can afford to offer them at a lower price because it paid less (probably 30% to 50% less). Brownish tinted diamonds go with any color of clothing, and they can be used to create distinctive designs (see figs. 5.3 & 5.7). A promotional term for light brownish-tinted diamonds is **champagne diamonds**. Darker brown diamonds are sometimes referred to as **cognac diamonds or fancy cognacs**.

How to Grade Color

Probably the best way to learn to color grade is to ask your jeweler to show you how. He or she will have some loose diamonds, a paper or plastic white grading tray, possibly a set of graded comparison diamonds called master stones and a good diffused (not bare) light source such as a daylight-equivalent fluorescent light. You might be surprised when the jeweler places the diamond upside down on the tray and has you look at the color through the pavilion (the backside of the diamond). This, however, is the most accurate way of seeing the fine nuances of color from one grade to another.

When you're judging diamonds for color, remember the following tips:

♦ Judge diamond color against a non-reflective white background. For example, you can fold a white business card in half and lay the diamond in the crease, or you can place the diamond in a white grading tray.

♦ Use comparison diamonds to determine a precise color grade. Even professional diamond graders realize that they cannot rely only on their color memory. They need master stones.

You can get a general idea of color without comparison stones. If you see an obvious yellowish tint when you view the stone through the side, then the stone is probably in the K to Z grade range.

♦ Make sure that the master stones and diamonds to be graded are clean. Dirt can affect the color grade.

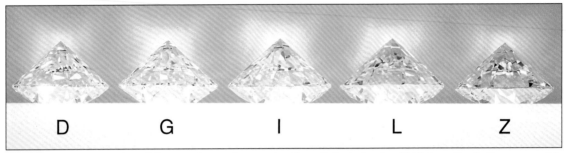

D   G   I   L   Z

Fig. 5.6 Diamonds of five different color grades ranging from D (colorless) to Z (light yellow). Do not use this photo to grade the color of your diamonds. The printing & developing processes and paper color usually alter the true color of gems in photographs. *Photo and diamonds from J. Landau, Inc.*

◆ Place your diamond both to the right and to the left of the master stones. It's normal for it to look lighter on one side than the other.

◆ Pay attention to the grading environment. Color grading can be affected by the lighting, the color of the surroundings and your clothes, the air quality, and the country you live in (the suns rays vary according to geographical regions) and the time of day and year. Yellow from your clothes, walls, gold mountings or sunlight can be reflected within the diamond.

◆ Be careful not to mistakenly downgrade larger diamonds. They often appear darker than small master stones of the same color grade because the color is easier to see.

◆ Remember that precise color grading can only be done with loose diamonds. The color of the metal surrounding diamonds set in jewelry influences the appearance of the diamonds. Consequently, their color can only be estimated.

Even though you should grade diamonds with a daylight equivalent fluorescent light, before buying a diamond, look at it under other lighting such as halogen spotlights, daylight by a window, overhead fluorescent lighting and light bulbs. Then you won't be disappointed when you get home and the diamond looks different than in the store. Lighting has an important impact on the appearance of gems. Smart sellers have you view stones under the most favorable lighting conditions. But you won't always be wearing your jewelry in the same environment.

How Objective are Color Grades?

Color grades are not as objective as people would like them to be. Even when the grader is someone as highly respected as the GIA, the color grade can be questioned. Russell Shor, senior editor of the *JCK (Jewelers' Circular Keystone* magazine), pointed out in their September 1987 issue that sometimes the grades of diamonds change when they are sent back to the GIA for re-examination. In 1995, Shor did a study of five diamonds which JCK sent to three major US gem labs. Only one of the diamonds received the same color and clarity grade from all three labs. For three of the stones, there was only a difference of one color and/or clarity grade, but for another, the difference was two clarity grades (*JCK.* July 1995, pp 60-66).

Usually grading differences involve borderline cases, and a change of more than one color or clarity grade is rare. However, the fact that no gem trade lab in the world will guarantee their grades or accept liability for their grading errors is a good indication that gemstone grading is subjective. Color measuring instruments exist, but normally grading has to be done by people because how they perceive the color is what's important. Some of the problems that make it so difficult for people to grade color objectively are:

♦ A color grade represents a range of color not an exact color. Therefore a G color can be almost an F or almost an H, and a G- and an H+ can look about the same.

♦ The size of master stones (color comparison diamonds) is usually much smaller than the stone being graded. Slight nuances of color are harder to detect in small stones than in large ones, so comparing stones of different sizes can be misleading.

♦ The proportions of master stones may be different than the stone being graded, creating differences in color perception.

♦ The shape and cutting style of master stones may be different from the diamond being graded. It's not easy to compare the color of an emerald-cut to that of a round brilliant master stone.

♦ Sometimes flaws in a diamond can affect the way color is perceived during grading.

♦ Sometimes a diamond is color-zoned, meaning it has two grades of color. A choice or average has to be made between the two colors.

In spite of the complexity of grading diamonds, professionals still often agree on color grades. You should, however, expect buyers and sellers to have strong disagreements, particularly when the color lies between two grades. Thousands of dollars can be at stake.

Does the lack of objectivity mean that color grades are worthless? Of course not. Thanks to the establishment of international color grading systems, it's easier now to do comparison shopping. You can discuss minute nuances of color and negotiate purchases with people thousands of miles away. However, when comparing prices, keep in mind that some sellers intentionally inflate color grades in order to make their diamonds appear to be a better buy than those of their competitors. Unfortunately, it's hard for lay people to tell when color grades have been misrepresented. That's why it's important to deal with trustworthy jewelers. For major purchases, it's advisable to get a grading report from a respected gem laboratory.

Gemological laboratories are aware of the limitations of diamond grading, so they normally have more than one person examine each diamond. You should be aware, too, of the limitations. If a jeweler tells you a stone is a G color and a gem lab calls it an H color, you shouldn't assume that the jeweler is incompetent or dishonest. If, however, a jeweler calls an unmounted K color diamond a G color, you would probably be better off doing business with another jeweler. An awareness of the limitations can also help you realize that some jewelers' prices may appear to be higher than other jewelers' when, in fact, they might be lower due to stricter grading. This is one reason why many jewelers don't like to quote prices over the phone. If they are strict graders, they know that their prices will be unfairly compared to other stores that overgrade their stones.

When you get a diamond back from an appraiser or gem lab, keep in mind that color grading is subjective. The report or certificate is not necessarily the last word. It is at best an independent, expert opinion.

Fig. 5.7 Light and dark brown diamonds, colorless diamonds and an orange sapphire in an interlocking platinum and 18K gold wedding ring set, which is shown in different views. Artist and designer, Eve J. Alfillé, created this distinctive ring set to look like a dump truck for a client in the trucking business. *Photo by Charles Hodges.*

Fig. 5.8 Tantalizing jeweled eye. The white of the eye is set with white diamonds, the iris with blue diamonds and the pupil with a black diamond. A 1.05 carat pear-shaped D flawless diamond forms the teardrop. This ingenious piece was designed and crafted by Sidney Mobell in platinum and 18K yellow gold. *Photo from Sidney Mobell.*

Diamond Fluorescence

If you were to place a diamond tennis bracelet under an ultraviolet light, many of the diamonds would probably have a noticeable blue glow and some would probably show hardly any glow or none. This is because diamonds are often fluorescent, which means they omit light when stimulated by UV lights or sunlight. Normally the fluorescence is blue but occasionally it's yellow, white or orange. The Hope Diamond has a distinctive red fluorescence.

There's a lot of misinformation about diamond fluorescence. For example, one dealer who advises consumers on the Internet and in a publication has stated, "If a diamond has fluorescence, it will have a cloudy or milky appearance, especially in sunlight." You can prove this is false by just looking at some transparent fluorescent diamonds. Conversely, there are cloudy diamonds that are not fluorescent. When buying a diamond, you should judge its transparency by its appearance, not by a lab report comment stating it's fluorescent. See Chapter 7 for tips on judging diamond transparency.

According to the *Rapaport Diamond Report*, the impact of blue fluorescence on price depends on its noticeability. "Fluorescence often adds value to lower color stones as it gives the stones a whiter, brighter appearance." For example, very strong blue fluorescence can add 0–3% to the value of I, J & K color stones. Strong and medium blue fluorescence may add 0–2%. Yellow fluorescence is considered negative and can discount the value of the stone by 5–10%.

In D–H color stones with a clarity of IF–VS, fluorescence of any color may have a negative impact. The discount may be 3–15% for very strong blue fluorescence. Strong blue fluorescence usually has no impact on the prices of F–H color diamonds with a clarity of SI_1–I_3.

The Spring-Summer 2000 issue of the "Professional Gemologist" newsletter has a good discussion on diamond fluorescence. In it, Tom Tashey, director of PGS (Professional Gem Sciences Inc.), states that when he began his gemological career at GIA's Gem Trade Laboratory (1975-1978), blue fluorescence was considered an asset to diamonds, even to those of top color and clarity. In fact GIA's diamond grading reports would include the following statement on reports of strongly fluorescent diamonds. "The ultraviolet fluorescence of this diamond will enhance its appearance in daylight." He suggests that the negative attitude towards blue fluorescence in top-color diamonds probably began when an investor at the market peak around 1979 tried to liquidate his "top quality investments" which had very strong blue fluorescence. The investor may have been told his diamonds had a hazy appearance and consequently were not worth near what he thought they were. Tashey adds that in his 25 years of grading diamonds, he's only seen 10–12 fluorescent stones with a hazy or cloudy transparency. Dealers don't normally send cloudy diamonds to labs for grading.

Tashey also presents another reason why fluorescent diamonds of top quality may be discounted today. He says diamond grading lights can emit a lot of UV radiation, so labs may overgrade some fluorescent diamonds viewed under these lights if no UV absorbing filter is used. The market may have responded by discounting them to compensate for overgrading.

If there's a question about the color grade of a fluorescent diamond, compare it next to a non-fluorescent diamond of the same color grade under a different light—one with hardly any UV radiation such as a diffused light bulb or a filtered fluorescent light. If the stones really have the same color grade, then the fluorescent stone should not appear to have more color than the other stone. For your protection, the grades should be ones established by an independent grading laboratory rather than by the seller.

Figs. 5.9–5.11 An array of natural color diamonds. The two photos at the bottom are enlarged views of a black diamond and a fancy intense green diamond (1.66 cts). *Photo and diamonds from Arthur Langerman.*

Fancy Color Diamonds

On April 28, 1987, a 0.95 carat diamond was sold for $880,000 at Christie's in New York. It contained two large flaws, one of which was a deep cavity in the table (top center facet) of the diamond. Despite its flaws and small size, it set a new world record per carat price for any gem sold at auction: $926,000 (reported by the summer 1987 issue of *Gems and Gemology*).

Why did that diamond command such a high price? Because its natural color was an extremely rare, deep, purplish-red. Color plays a significant role in determining the price of a diamond.

Many people are surprised to learn that diamonds come in a wide selection of colors including various shades of green, orange, yellow, blue, purple and pink. But such diamonds are not very common, so they have been given a special name—**fancy color diamonds**, meaning diamonds with a natural body color other than light yellow, light brown or light gray.

What color diamond, then, is best? That's a matter of personal opinion. What color diamond is most expensive? Currently the answer is purplish red; but natural-color green, blue and purplish pink are also unusually expensive as you can see from Table 51 on the next page. It lists the highest per-carat prices paid at auction for diamonds in various color categories.

Fig. 5.12 Fancy yellow and pink diamonds in a flower brooch by Cynthia Renée Co. *Photo by Robert Weldon.*

You don't have to pay such high prices to enjoy colored diamonds. You can find fancy yellow diamonds at prices slightly above H and I color diamonds. Brown diamonds are available for half the price of I color diamonds of the same size and quality. There's also the option of buying treated diamonds. According to *The Guide Reference Manual* for 1999, irradiated diamonds ⅓ ct and up sell for about 10–20% more than M color diamonds. This includes irradiated blue, green and orange diamonds. Irradiation is usually done on diamonds of M color or below. Since there's a cost involved in treating these diamonds and the treatment may make the diamond more marketable, the prices charged for these diamonds are usually above the price of an M color diamond, an extremely low price compared to natural fancy color diamonds.

As you look at Table 6.1, you'll notice terms such as "fancy" and "fancy vivid." These are color grades established by the GIA. Fancy vivid is the highest color grade, followed by fancy intense, fancy deep, fancy and fancy dark. GIA colored diamond grades are explained in the Winter 1994 issue of *Gems & Gemology* (pp. 220–242).

Some people within the trade think that the GIA colored-diamond terminology is either confusing or not descriptive enough. For example, one colored-diamond dealer said he has 10 stones with the same color description—fancy yellow—that all have different colors. Some appraisers wonder why colored-diamond terminology isn't the same as that used for other colored stones such as rubies and sapphires.

Table 5.1 Highest per-carat prices paid at auction for diamonds with different natural colors

Color Grade and Color	Carat Weight	Shape & Cutting Style	Date of Sale	Per Carat Price
Red				
Fancy purplish red	0.95	round brilliant	Apr 1987	$926,315
Fancy red	0.25	oval brilliant	Oct 1996	$326,000
Orange-Yellow				
Fancy intense orange-yellow	4.77	rectangular cut	Nov 1990	$821,803
Pink				
Fancy intense purplish pink	7.37	emerald cut	Nov 1995	$819,201
Fancy purplish pink	4.92	emerald cut	Apr 1995	$425,304
Green				
Fancy vivid green	0.90	round brilliant	Oct 1999	$736,111
Fancy yellowish green	3.02	pear brilliant	Apr 1988	$564,569
Blue				
Fancy deep blue	4.37	oval brilliant	Nov 1995	$568,740
Fancy deep blue	13.49	emerald cut	Apr 1995	$554.670
Yellow		marquise		
Fancy vivid yellow	13.83	antique brilliant	Apr 1997	$238,792
Fancy intense yellow	18.49	pear brilliant	June 1990	$203,461
Orange		cushion		
Fancy vivid orange	5.54	modified brilliant	Oct 1997	$238,718
Fancy intense yellow-orange	8.93	pear brilliant	May 1988	$211,113
Colorless				
(D IF)	52.59	rectangular cut	Apr 1988	$142,232
(D IF)	101.84	pear brilliant	Nov 1990	$125,294

1 ct D flawless round diamonds have sold for as much as $63,000 (March 1980)

Purple				
Fancy reddish purple	0.54	round brilliant	Apr 1987	$122,222
Fancy purple	1.04	bullet step cut	Nov 1990	$94,240
Brown				
Fancy orangish brown	8.91	octagon step cut	Apr 1987	$9,259
Fancy reddish brown	1.14	round brilliant	Oct 1988	$6,754
Black				
Fancy black	46.53	circular briolette	Oct 1996	$2,418
Fancy black	67.50	cushion brilliant	Dec 1990	$1,466

The information in the above chart is from pages 122 and 123 of *Collecting and Classifying Coloured Diamonds* by Stephen C. Hofer, Jewelry International (Dec/Jan 92/93), Christie's, Sotheby's, and the *Auction Market Resource* by Gail Levine.

Fig. 5.13 Above: A 3-carat fancy intense yellow radiant cut diamond in a platinum and 18K gold man's ring. *Photo & ring from Vivid Collection.*

Fig. 5.14 Right: matching fancy yellow diamonds, 8.59 cts & 8.78 cts, both internally flawless. *Photo and diamonds from Vivid Collection.*

The term "fancy" used to be reserved for diamonds with highly-valued colors such as red, blue, green, pink, purple, orange and yellow. It wasn't normally associated with colors like black and brown as it is today. Nowadays, "fancy" is even used to describe low-grade translucent diamonds that are milky white. Even though these diamonds may be called fancy white on lab reports, this doesn't make them valuable. You should no longer assume that the grade "fancy" necessarily means a diamond is unusually valuable.

When you buy colored diamonds, you should be more concerned with their actual appearance than with a color grade on a lab report. You're buying a gemstone, not a piece of paper. Remember to look at diamonds under a variety of lights. Sometimes they seem to have a color change as you look at them under fluorescent lights, halogen spotlights and in daylight. To appreciate the beauty of colored diamonds you need to view them firsthand. Additional information on colored diamonds can be found in *Collecting and Classifying Coloured Diamonds* by Stephen C. Hofer and the companion AMR Millennium Edition of the December 2000 Auction Market Resource. For information on purchasing the Auction Market Resource, call 718 897-7305.

Diamond Color Treatments

Currently, there are two principal methods of permanently changing the color of a diamond:
♦ Irradiation + heating
♦ High pressure high temperature heat treatment (HPHT treatment)

Both of these treatment processes are considered legitimate as long as they're disclosed to buyers. Unfortunately, some people try to pass off treated diamonds as naturally colored in order to get a higher price. So before investing a high sum of money in a fancy-color diamond, have the stone tested by a reputable gem laboratory for possible color treatment. Also have the seller write on the receipt that the diamond is natural and not treated. There's nothing wrong with color treatments as long as you are told about them and not charged natural color prices.

Not all diamond color treatments are permanent and legitimate. Many are temporary and done only with the intention of deceiving the buyer. Occasionally the girdle or back of the diamond is coated with a chemical or plastic to make it look less yellow. Sometimes bits of carbon paper under the prongs or a few dots of ink on the girdle are used to improve the color. In one instance a 9 1/2 carat fancy pink diamond at a major auction house was switched and replaced with a stone coated with pink nail polish. To avoid these deceptive tricks, deal with reputable jewelers.

Why Color-Treated Diamonds Aren't as Well Accepted as Other Treated Gems

Most rubies and sapphires are heat treated at high temperatures to improve their color, and this is considered a standard trade practice. Red tourmaline is commonly irradiated to intensify its color, and this is also considered normal.

Color-treated diamonds, however, are not as well accepted. Three reasons for this are:

♦ Unlike many other gems, there's an ample supply of attractive, untreated diamonds.

♦ Diamonds cost a lot more than most other gems, so more money is at stake. When the prices of rubies and sapphires approach those of top quality diamonds, high-temperature heat treatment becomes less acceptable.

♦ Unlike colored-gem dealers, most diamond dealers don't stock color-treated stones, so they view them as a threat to their business. Treatments are not always disclosed; treated gems confuse consumers, and they can reduce the price of natural-color gems.

A good example of this occurred in the mid- to late- 1970's. Thailand began heat treating low-grade Sri Lankan sapphire on a large scale and the treatment was not disclosed to buyers. Prices of natural-color sapphires dropped when they had to compete with treated stones, which had better color and clarity.

So far, color treatments have not affected the prices of natural diamonds. Fancy color diamonds are worth far more than their treated counterparts. A $2000, irradiated green diamond might sell for over $200,000 if it were natural. Prices of high-pressure high-temperature treated diamonds (HPHT-treated diamonds) have not been established yet because they're relatively new. The colorless type were first introduced to the trade in 1999. Trade magazines have stated they're being sold to jewelers for about 15% less than natural-color diamonds. This is high considering that these treated diamonds are produced from brown diamonds. But as more HPHT-treated diamonds enter the market and competition increases, prices for them will most likely decrease.

HPHT-treated yellowish-green diamonds were introduced at the beginning of 2000. In October 2000, the trade press announced that the General Electric Company was able to produce HPHT blue and pink diamonds. The producers will naturally try to get the highest price possible for these diamonds. They claim their treatment process is as natural as the process of cutting and polishing a diamond and that it's just an extension of the high temperatures diamonds are exposed to when formed naturally.

Gems are also subjected to radiation in nature, but the trade does not view irradiation treatment as a natural process. According to Arthur Langerman, a Belgium dealer who specializes in colored diamonds, irradiated and heat-treated diamonds just imitate the real thing. He says that treated diamonds have a value to the people who sell them but not to the rest of the trade. To illustrate this, he said that he'd received a few irradiated diamonds instead of payment a few years ago. He still has them because he hasn't found anyone who wants to buy them. Auction houses wouldn't even take them for zero.

Langerman poses the question, "If you have $100,000 to spend, what would you buy—a natural white diamond or a diamond that has been treated from brown to white?" He responds that he would never spend that money on a diamond that has been artificially treated.

6

Judging Cut Quality

I f it's not cut right, a flawless D color diamond might be considered a reject by a diamond dealer. A poor cut can make a diamond look dull, glassy, bulky and too small for its weight. A good cut can increase its brilliance, sparkle, durability and aesthetic appeal.

The term *cut* is sometimes confusing because it has a variety of meanings. Jewelers use it to refer to:

♦ The **shape** of a gemstone (e.g. round or oval)
♦ The **cutting style** (e.g. brilliant or step cut, single or full cut)
♦ The **proportions** of a stone (e.g. big or small table facet, deep or shallow pavilion)
♦ The **finish** of a stone (e.g. polishing marks or smooth flawless surface, misshapen or symmetrical facets)

We'll be focusing on diamond proportions and finish, which are also called the **make** of a stone. Shape and cutting style were discussed in Chapter 4.

The main purpose of this chapter is to help you learn how to judge cut visually, a skill not often taught to consumers. You should evaluate diamonds mainly on the basis of their appearance instead of using only grades and proportion measurements.

Diamond grading reports don't give you a complete picture of a diamond and they don't have brilliance grades. You have to look at a diamond first-hand to see how faceting, proportioning, shape, color, clarity and transparency interact to give beauty and life to a stone. You'll appreciate your diamonds more if you can determine visually why they're well cut.

This chapter will also help you interpret some of the cut data found on appraisals and lab reports. This will enable you to use these reports as a confirmation that you've chosen a good diamond. However, even if you read this chapter, you'll need professional assistance. But in order to determine if a salesperson is competent, you should know some basics about assessing cut.

Judging the Face-Up View

You should evaluate diamond brilliance both with the naked eye and a 10-power magnifier. Stones should be lit from above with a diffused light source such as a fluorescent lamp—not with a bare light bulb or spotlight. Bare light accentuates sparkle, but it can create dark shadows and it is not as even and broad as light which passes through a translucent bulb or material.

Good diamonds display brilliance throughout the stone (6.1, 6.3 & 6.5–7). They shouldn't have dark or washed-out areas which allow you to see through the bottom of the stone. The diamond in figure 6.2 has a dark center because its **pavilion** (bottom part) was cut too deep. Such

Fig. 6.1 A diamond with good brilliance

Fig. 6.2 A dark center and a large table

Fig. 6.3 A well-cut marquise

Fig. 6.4 A dark bow tie

Fig. 6.5 A well-cut oval, a Gabrielle™. *Photo from Suberi Bros.*

Fig. 6.6 A Gabrielle™ octagonal square brilliant cut. *Photo from Suberi Bros.*

diamonds are called **nailheads**. Fancy cuts such as the pear, marquise, oval or emerald cut may display a dark **bow tie** as in figure 6.4 when the pavilion facets are not properly angled. The larger and darker the bow tie, the less desirable the stone. Most fancy-shaped diamonds have at

Fig. 6.7 Emerald cut with good brilliance

Fig. 6.8 A distracting black cross

least a slight bow tie, but when it is so pronounced that it is distracting, the bow tie lowers the value of the stone. Occasionally other dark patterns such as a cross are visible (fig. 6.8).

Sometimes the face-up view displays a white circle resembling a skinny donut (figs. 6.9 6.10. In the trade, this is called a **fisheye**. It's caused by the reflection of the girdle (outer diamond edge) when the pavilion is too shallow. The thicker and more prominent the white circle, the poorer the cut is. Besides looking bad, fisheye diamonds usually lack the brilliance of well-cut diamonds.

Fig. 6.9 A fisheye in a diamond with a shallow pavilion

Fig. 6.10 A less noticeable fisheye beneath a large table facet

When the **crown** (top portion) of a round brilliant diamond is too high, the upper girdle and bezel facets will look crinkled (figs. 6.11 & 6.12). Eight flower-like patterns may be visible near the corners of the **table** (the big, top, center facet forming an octagon on a round stone). High-crown diamonds look small for their weight when set and may have reduced brilliance.

Diamonds in antique pieces should not be judged by the same standards as the modern round brilliant. Old mine and old European cuts typically have very high crowns (see Chapter 4). It wasn't until after about 1910 that the modern round brilliant was developed from theoretical calculations of optimal diamond brilliance.

Fig. 6.11 Face-up view of a diamond with a high crown.

Fig. 6.12 Another diamond with a high crown. This one has a smaller table.

When judging the face-up view, you should also consider the **table size** (the diameter of the large central facet on the top of a stone). If it's too large, the diamond won't have much sparkle or **fire** (flashes of rainbow colors, which are technically referred to as **dispersion**). If the table is too small, the diamond will not display enough brilliance, and it will probably look small for its weight. Diamonds with small tables often have high crowns and those with large tables tend to have thin crowns.

Opinions differ as to what is the best table size for a diamond. Diamond cutters in Europe have tended to prefer bigger tables than American diamond cutters. Some Americans feel that the ideal table width for a round diamond is 53% of the girdle diameter. Some Europeans might slightly downgrade a 53% table. Perhaps most jewelers would agree that the table width should be from 53% to less than 67% of the girdle diameter. Figure 6.13 illustrates four different table sizes. The table size of a round diamond is calculated by dividing the maximum table width by the average girdle diameter or width to get a percentage. It's also possible for professionals to visually estimate table size. Consumers can learn to recognize the difference between large and small tables, but for fine distinctions of table size, it's best to refer to a lab report or appraisal for the table size ratio.

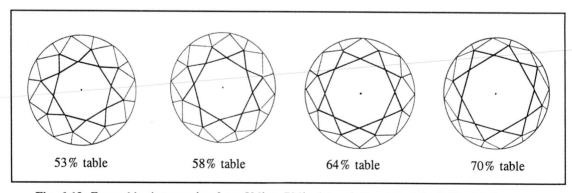

53% table   58% table   64% table   70% table

Fig. 6.13 Four table sizes ranging from 53% to 70% of the girdle width. The 70%-table is too large for good sparkle and fire. *Diagrams courtesy of the Gemological Institute of America.*

The **symmetry** of the stone should also be noted. No diamond is 100% symmetrical, but when the diamond looks lopsided or the major facets are strikingly irregular, then it is considered unacceptable. Symmetry is less important than factors such as pavilion depth, crown height and table size. Poor symmetry can be distracting, but it doesn't necessarily keep a diamond from displaying a high degree of brilliance, sparkle and fire.

Judging the Profile

When you buy a diamond, be sure to look at its profile with and without magnification. The side view will show you:

♦ If the crown is too thick or too thin.

♦ If the pavilion is too deep or too shallow.

♦ If the girdle is too thick or too thin.

♦ If the diamond is too bulky or too flat.

Figure 6.14 reviews some diamond terminology and serves as an example of a well-proportioned round brilliant.

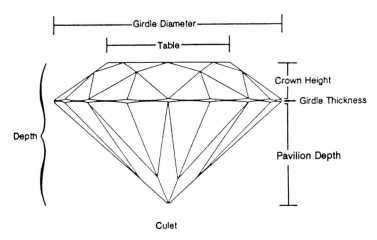

Fig. 6.14 Profile of a well-cut round brilliant diamond

Measure the depth and girdle diameter of the diagrammed diamond and then divide the depth by the girdle diameter. The depth should be about 60% of the diameter, a good ratio for a round diamond. The technical term for this ratio is **total depth percentage** or simply **depth percentage**. When judging a fancy-shape diamond, divide the depth by the width. The GIA suggests that the depth is normally in the range of 55% to 65% of the width of the diamond.

Occasionally a customer will ask for a diamond with a 59% or 60% depth because he may have been told that this is the ideal depth for a diamond. There are two problems with this approach. First, the total depth percentage does not indicate if a diamond is well cut. A fisheye stone with a high crown can have a 60% depth percentage. Second, you won't learn to make good

Fig. 6.15 A very thin crown. This diamond will not have much sparkle or fire.

Fig. 6.16 Lengthwise view of a marquise with a thin crown and an unusually thick girdle

visual judgments if you rely solely on numerical data when buying gems. In fact, most diamond dealers do not know the total depth percentage of all of their diamonds, nor do they ask their suppliers to indicate it.

Appraisers and gem laboratories include numerical data on their reports because they must provide objective information about the stones they grade. Unfortunately, many reports neglect to include relevant information such as the crown height and pavilion depth percentage.

The **crown height percentage** is calculated by dividing the crown height by the girdle diameter (girdle width for fancy cuts like the marquise). The stone in the diagram of figure 6.14 has about a 16% crown height percentage. You don't need to know this percentage when buying a diamond. You can tell if the crown is too low by looking at the stone from the side and comparing it to the profile of well-cut stones. In addition, the stone will have reduced fire and sparkle. A lay person can see that the crowns in figures 6.15 and 6.16, for example, are too low. The round brilliant in figure 6.15 has a crown height percentage of about 7%. The marquise would have to be viewed widthwise to make proportion calculations. Many radiants and princess cuts have extremely thin crowns.

The most obvious sign of high crowns is the crinkled appearance of the facets in the face-up view (figs. 6.11 & 6.12). The **crown angle**, another measure found on some appraisals and lab reports, can be an indication of crown height. A crown angle greater than 40° suggest a high crown. A stone with a crown angle of less than 30° is likely to have a thin crown. The American Gem Society considers a crown angle in the range of 33.7° – 35.8° to be ideal for standard round brilliant cut diamonds.

The **pavilion depth percentage** can be easily judged from the face-up view. If the stone has a dark center or fisheye, there are problems with the pavilion angles and depth. If the pavilion depth of a round brilliant is 40% or less, the stone will have a fisheye. When the pavilion depth is 49% or more, the stone will have a dark center. The American Gem Society defines the ideal pavilion depth percentage range as 42.2% – 43.8% for standard round brilliant cuts.

The pavilion depth percentage is probably the most important proportion factor because it provides clues about the overall brilliance of a diamond. If the table is too large or the crown is too thin, a stone can still look brilliant, provided the pavilion is properly proportioned. The diamond will just lack sparkle and fire. However, if the pavilion is too shallow, the stone will look watery and lifeless.

Fig. 6.17 A well-cut faceted girdle

Fig. 6.18 A very thick faceted girdle

The **girdle** (the rim around the diamond which separates the crown from the pavilion) must be evaluated from the side view. A well-cut girdle will not be:

♦ Too thick or too thin
♦ Very uneven in thickness
♦ Wavy or slanted
♦ Rough or bearded (with microscopic hair-like fractures along the girdle)

Diamonds with thin girdles are hard to set and easy to chip. Diamonds with thick girdles have reduced brilliance, look smaller than they weigh, and are also hard to set. The judgment of girdle thickness is best done with the eye, with and without magnification. If the girdle looks like a wide band encircling the diamond, it is probably too thick. If the girdle is sharp and you can hardly see it, then it is probably too thin. Figures 6.17 to 6.20 provide examples of different types of girdles. As you examine diamond girdles you will notice three types:

♦ **Faceted** (figs. 6.17, 6.18, 6.21, 6.24 and 6.26)
♦ **Bruted**, with a frosty or waxy look (figs. 6.19 and 6.23)
♦ **Polished** with no facets, looking like a clear continuous rim of glass going around the diamond (fig. 6.25)

Fig. 6.19 A rough bruted girdle with slight bearding and a natural (the non-rough part of the girdle)

Fig. 6.20 An irregular girdle that is part polished and part bruted

Figures 6.21 to 6.26 will give you additional practice at evaluating girdles and the profile view of diamonds.

Fig. 6.21 An extremely thick girdle on a bulky-looking round brilliant. This stone will look small for its weight face up.

Fig. 6.22 An irregular girdle on a diamond with a large table and a shallow pavilion. Same stone as in figs. 6.10 and 6.20.

Fig. 6.23 A thin, bruted girdle on a round brilliant with a high crown. This is the same stone as in figure 6.12.

Fig. 6.24 A chunky marquise with a very thick girdle. Its bulging pavilion reduces brilliance and creates a bow tie. Face-up this stone looks small for its weight

Fig. 6.25 A princess cut with a thin crown and polished girdle. In the face-up view, this stone does not have much sparkle or fire because of its very large table and low crown. It does, however, have acceptable brilliance.

Fig. 6.26 The table of this stone is a little too wide for it to be classified as an "ideal cut." Nevertheless, it's a well-proportioned diamond with good brilliance and sparkle.

Bruted girdles should be smooth and precision cut. If they are rough, as in figure 6.19, they can trap dirt, giving the girdle a gray, dark look. Sometimes, girdles have fringes looking like whiskers and hairs. They are appropriately called **bearded girdles** and can lower the clarity grade of diamonds—especially those of high clarity.

"Ideal-Cut" Diamonds

A lay person would probably assume that an "ideal-cut" diamond is one with the best possible proportions. Any diamond with different proportions would be inferior. In the American jewelry trade, though, the term "ideal cut" is applied to round diamonds with proportions similar to those proposed by Marcel Tolkowsky, a mathematician and diamond cutter who is sometimes referred to as the "father" of the American brilliant cut.

Fig. 6.27 An AGS-quality, "ideal-cut" diamond

Fig. 6.28 Profile of the same "ideal cut"

The exact proportions of the "ideal-cut" vary depending on whom you talk to. For example, some say the ideal table size is 53%, others say 55%, and many prefer to indicate a range such as 53–57%. However, now that the American Gem Society (AGS) has established a reputable gem laboratory that grades the cut of round diamonds, more and more trade professionals are accepting their criteria for defining the American "ideal cut." Nowadays, dealers usually send "ideal-cut" diamonds to the AGS laboratory so they can get the coveted cut grade of 0 on a grading report. Stones with a 0 cut grade sell at premiums of up to 15%. The GIA doesn't grade cut, and their diamond grading reports don't include proportion information about the pavilion, which is probably the main determinant of diamond brilliance.

The AGS standards for grading round diamond proportions are listed on the next page. Besides receiving a 0 proportions grade, diamonds must get a polish grade of 0 and a symmetry grade of 0 to be called an AGS ideal cut. This means that polish and symmetry characteristics such as misshapen facets are extremely difficult to locate under 10-power magnification.

American Gem Society (AGS) Proportion Standards for Rounds

On a scale of 0 to 10, 0 is the AGS ideal and 10 is the worst. An AGS ideal-cut round diamond is one that receives a 0 grade in all of the categories below.

Average Crown Angle

	AGS Grade
28.3 and less	10
28.4 to 29.1	9
29.2 to 29.6	8
29.7 to 30.1	7
30.2 to 30.6	6
30.7 to 31.1	5
31.2 to 31.6	4
31.7 to 32.6	3
32.7 to 33.6	2
32.7 to 33.8	1
33.7 to 35.8	**0**
35.9 to 36.3	1
36.4 to 36.8	2
37.4 to 37.8	3
37.9 to 38.3	5
38.4 to 38.8	6
38.9 to 39.3	7
39.4 to 39.8	8
39.9 and greater	10

Average Table Diameter %

	AGS Grade
46.3 and smaller	10
46.4 to 47.3	9
47.4 to 48.3	8
48.4 to 49.3	7
49.4 to 50.3	5
50.4 to 51.3	3
51.4 to 52.3	1
52.4 to 57.5	**0**
57.8 to 59.5	1
59.6 to 61.5	2
61.6 to 63.5	3
63.6 to 65.5	4
65.6 to 67.5	5
67.8 to 69.5	6
69.6 to 71.5	7
71.8 to 73.5	8
73.6 to 75.5	9
75.6 to 75.5	10

Average Pavilion Depth %

39.4 and less	9–10
39.5 to 40.1	8
40.2 to 40.6	7
40.7 to 41.1	5
41.2 to 41.6	4
41.7 to 42.1	2
42.2 to 43.8	**0**
43.9 to 44.3	1
44.4 to 44.8	2
44.9 to 45.5	5
45.6 to 46.5	6
46.6 to 47.5	8
47.6 to 48.5	9
48.6+	10

Average Girdle Thickness

Extremely thin	7
Very thin	1
Thin, Medium, &	0
Slightly thick	0
Thick	3
Very thick	5
Extremely thick	7–10

Culet Size (overall average)

Pointed, very small,	0
small, medium	0
Slightly large	1
Large	3
Very large	5
Extremely large	7–10

GIA Cut Grading Standards for Round Brilliant Diamonds

The GIA Diamond Grading Course (1994) presents four different make (cut quality) categories for standard round diamonds. Even though the GIA Gem Trade Lab doesn't grade cut on its lab reports, many appraisers use the GIA cut quality classes to establish cut grades for their appraisals.

CLASS 1, Top quality, Excellent
Crown angle 34⁰-35⁰
Pavilion depth% . . . . close to 43%
Table size % . . . . . 53-60% of girdle diameter
        (In stones up to 0.50 ct, it goes up to 61-62%)
Girdle . . . . medium-slightly thick
Culet . . . . none-medium
Finish (symmetry and polish) . very good to excellent

CLASS 2, Good quality
Crown angle 32-34⁰
Pavilion depth % 42-44%
Table size . . . . 60 to 64%
Girdle . . . . thin / thick
Culet . . . . slightly large
Finish . . . . good

CLASS 3, Average quality
Crown angle . . . . . . 30-32⁰ or 37⁰
Pavilion depth% 41-46%
Table size . . . . 65-70% or 51-52%
Girdle . . . . very thin / very thick

Culet . . . . large
Finish . . . . fair

CLASS 4, Low Quality
Crown angle . . . . below 30⁰ or above 37⁰
Pavilion depth % . . below 41% or above 46%
Table size % . . . . above 70% or below 51%
Girdle . . . . extremely thin / extremely thick
Culet . . . . very large
Finish . . . . poor

Brilliant Cut Proportion Standards of the Belgium Diamond High Council (HRD)

Criteria	Not Good	Good	Very Good	Good	Not Good
crown angle	below 27°	27° – 30.6°	30.7° – 37.7°	37.8° – 40.6°	above 40.6%
table width %	below 51%	51 – 52%	53 – 66%	67 – 70%	above 70%
crown height %	below 9%	9 – 10.5%	11 – 16%	16.5 – 18%	above 18%
girdle thickness	extremely thin	very thin	thin & medium	thick & very thick	extremely thick
pavilion depth %	below 40%	40 – 41%	41.5 – 45%	45.5 – 46.5%	above 46.5%
total depth %	below 53%	53 – 55.4%	55.5 – 63.9%	64 – 66.9%	above 66.9%
pavilion angle	below 38.5°	38.5° – 39.5°	39.6° – 42.2°	42.3° – 43.1°	above 43.1°

Additional condition for the diamond in order to be considered good or very good: the reflection of the girdle should not be visible through the table-facet by perpendicular observation. (I.C. FISH EYE EFFECT)

Fig. 6.29 Note the high brilliance of this Gabrielle® diamond. It has more facets and different proportion requirements than the standard round brilliant cut. *Photo from Suberi Bros.*

"Ideal cuts" normally cost more than the average diamond because more weight is lot from the rough, and more skill and time are required to cut them. Many stores do not stock "ideal cuts" but they can order them for you. It can be difficult to find "ideal cuts" in sizes less than a half of a carat. Figures 6.27 and 6.28 show the face-up and profile view of an "ideal cut" diamond with a 55% table. Compare the symmetry and precision of the cutting to that of most other diamonds and you'll understand why some people are willing to spend more for an "ideal cut."

Some cutters prefer diamonds with a slightly larger table than the AGS ideal cut and will cut them with the same degree of precision; the larger table makes the diamond appear a little bigger, yet it doesn't reduce brilliance. It's a matter of opinion which diamond proportions are best. There are ranges of acceptability and unacceptability, but even these can be debated.

Sometimes, sellers of AGS ideal cuts will try to prove that their diamonds are the absolute best cuts by comparing them to poor quality cuts or to well-cut diamonds with a lower transparency. They'll have you note the difference in brilliance, which will most likely be obvious. However, you probably wouldn't see a difference if you were to look an AGS ideal cut next to a highly transparent, precision-cut diamond with say a 60% table, which is too large for the diamond to be classified as an AGS ideal cut.

Another example of an attractive diamond that is not an AGS ideal cut is the Gabrielle® shown in figure 6.29. If you were to see it in person, you'd be impressed by its brilliance, fire and sparkle. It was created by Gabriel Tolkowsky the master diamond cutter who designed and cut the "Golden Jubilee" and the Centenary Diamond. His great uncle was Marcel Tolkowsky, who established in 1919 the proportion parameters on which the AGS ideal cut is based.

In short, AGS ideal cuts are not the only beautiful diamonds. When you shop, look at other well-cut diamonds too, compare them side by side and see what looks best to you.

Judging Brilliance

Sometimes we get so involved in analyzing the color, clarity and cut of a diamond that we forget to notice if the diamond is brilliant or not. A diamond can be well cut, yet not brilliant. Color, shape, cutting style, polish, inclusions, transparency and the chemical composition of the diamond also affect its brilliance. If, however, a diamond is highly brilliant, one can assume it's well-proportioned.

Learning to recognize degrees of diamond brilliance is a challenge and can best be done by comparing diamonds and other gemstones of varying brilliance. The stones should first be cleaned and then viewed face up. When dull and glassy stones are viewed next to brilliant stones, the differences become obvious. It's hard to explain brilliance with words, but it can be described as a mirror-like quality resulting from the reflection of light off the surface and interior of a stone. The greater the light return, the greater the brilliance. Diamonds have the potential of displaying a brilliance unmatched by any other gemstone. This is because of their optical properties and their superior hardness, which allows them to have an unusually high polish.

Judge brilliance both with the naked eye and with a hand magnifier (loupe). Differences in brilliance are easier to notice and appreciate under ten-power magnification.

Make sure that you compare diamonds under equivalent lighting conditions, but look at them together under different types of overhead light such as fluorescent tubes, halogen spotlights and daylight near a window. This way you'll know in advance what the diamonds will look like when worn outside the store. Also examine diamonds under the light and away from it. The closer diamonds are to the light, the more brilliant they will look.

Before buying a diamond, take a moment to simply ask yourself if it looks brilliant, both with the naked eye and under magnification. When you pay diamond prices, you want to get diamond brilliance. To compare subtle nuances of diamond brilliance, you need a reference standard—a well-cut, brilliant comparison diamond along with the assistance of a competent salesperson. The consumer's eye cannot remember fine differences of brilliance when going from store to store to shop for diamonds.

Judging Cut with the Eye Instead of with Numbers

When I worked in the diamond trade, I often had to sort parcels of diamonds. They were normally presorted for general color and size but needed to be separated into different price categories according to clarity, transparency and cut quality. I had about 3–5 seconds to evaluate each stone. There wasn't time to compute the proportions of each diamond. I had to learn to judge cut with the eye because that's the fastest way to get a general assessment of a stone's cut quality.

You don't need a gemologist diploma or a list of proportion measurements to tell the difference between a well-cut stone and one that's poorly cut. You can learn to do this with your eye and it's to your advantage to learn how. Here's why:

◆ **You'll be able to spot cutting defects that may not be indicated on grading reports or mentioned by salespeople.** Many diamond reports, such as those issued by the GIA, leave out information on the pavilion depth, which indicates whether the stone has a dark center or a fish eye effect. Even though a total depth percentage is normally included, this tells you little about the depth of the pavilion or the height of the crown. It's easy to visually tell if the crown or pavilion is too low or too high.

◆ **There are no agreed upon proportion standards for fancy shapes.** You have to look at the stone to determine if there's brilliance throughout the stone or a noticeable bow tie.

◆ With the exception of the center stone for a ring, **most of the diamonds you buy will be mounted and will not come with lab documents and proportion measurements.** You'll have to look at the stones in semi-mounts, necklaces, bracelets and brooches to determine if they're well cut. What's the point of buying an "ideal-cut" diamond and then placing it in a mounting with shallow or deep-cut small diamonds?

♦ **You'll have more fun shopping if you consider diamonds in terms of their brilliance and sparkle instead of numbers.** Some people turn diamond-buying into a frustrating experience by going from store to store asking if they have a stone with a specific angle or proportion measurement. These shoppers usually never find the diamond that meets all of their specifications and they don't experience the pleasure of looking at a range of beautiful diamonds.

♦ **The ability to judge cut visually will help you compare prices more accurately.** Poor cuts may be discounted as much as 50%. Ideal cuts may carry premiums of 10–15%. Consequently there may be a major difference in value between two diamonds that have the same weight, shape, color and clarity if their cut quality is different.

♦ The most important reason to learn to judge cut with your eye is so that **you'll be able to appreciate your diamond more after you purchase it.** How can you appreciate something you don't comprehend? When you see well-cut diamonds contrasted to inferior cuts, it's easier to understand the importance of cut. Knowing why your diamond is well cut will help you realize why it's special.

Reread this chapter; then cover up the photo captions. See if you can determine which diamonds are well cut and which aren't and why. When you go shopping, ask the salespeople to show you the difference between a good and poorly cut diamond. They don't have to mention numbers. They can use terms such as high crown, shallow pavilion, thick girdle, lopsided table and excess weight. Not only will you learn more about diamond cut, you'll learn if you're dealing with someone who's knowledgeable and who can help you select a good quality diamond.

After you select a diamond, proportion measurements can be useful. They help you confirm that you made a wise choice and they provide good documentation for your diamond. If you ever need your diamond replaced by an insurance company or a store, the more information you have about the diamond, the better. Legally, insurance companies only have to replace it with the quality indicated on your appraisal, lab report and/or receipt. If proportion measurements are not indicated, it's to their financial advantage to replace your diamond with the least expensive quality cut. If you ever suspect that your diamond has been switched, proportion measurements can be a useful means of distinguishing your diamonds from others.

It's pointless to invest a lot of money in a diamond whose beauty is diminished by major cutting defects. So pay attention to cut quality as you shop for diamonds. If you can recognize a fine-cut, brilliant diamond with your eyes, you're well on your way to spotting value.

7

Judging Clarity & Transparency

I magine looking into a colorless kaleidoscope and seeing things resembling miniature galaxies, abstract sculptures, feathers, dots, fishing lines, eroded canyons, or diamond crystals. That's what it can be like to look at a diamond through a microscope.

When you try to find the forms within a stone and marks on its exterior, you are analyzing its clarity. **Clarity** is the degree to which a stone is free from external marks called **blemishes** and internal features called **inclusions**. Together they represent the **clarity characteristics** or **clarity features** of the stone. You may be more familiar with terms such as "flaws," "imperfections" or "defects." Gemologists prefer not to use these terms because of their negative connotations. This book sometimes uses the term "flaw" because it's short and easy for a lay person to understand.

It can be to your advantage to buy a diamond with inclusions and blemishes. They can be proof that it is authentic, untreated and of natural origin. They can act as a fingerprint and help protect you from having your diamond switched. They can lower the price of the diamond without affecting its beauty. They can make you feel your diamond is special. So, if you're buying a diamond for personal enjoyment, don't worry about how to find a flawless one; instead just be concerned about flaws that will make your diamond less attractive and less durable. In addition, learn how clarity affects diamond value so that you can accurately compare prices.

Examining Diamonds for Clarity

To examine a stone for clarity you need a ten-power magnifier, a lint free cloth and a light source with a translucent shade or with a bulb that's frosted—not bare. An ordinary fluorescent desk lamp will do. Tweezers or a stone-holder is also helpful. Jewelers often use a hand magnifier called a loupe (fig. 7.1). For those interested in owning a loupe, the business section of the phone book has stores listed under "Jewelers' Supplies & Findings." First verify that they have a fully corrected, ten-power, triplet loupe. The loupe salesman or a jeweler can show you some ways of holding and using it

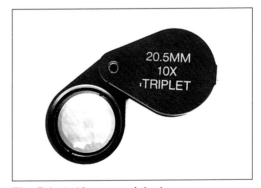

Fig. 7.1 A 10-power triplet loupe

and help you select the model that is the most comfortable and clear. Plan on paying at least $25 for a good loupe. Cheaper types, which are not fully corrected, tend to distort objects.

When using a ten-power loupe, hold it about 1/2 to 1 inch (13–25 mm.) away from the stone to bring it into focus. If you're examining a large stone, hold the loupe close to one eye (about 1 or 2 inches or 25–50 mm. from the eye) keeping both eyes open. The closer the loupe is to your eye, the greater your field of vision will be. Often it's easier for lay people to examine stones through a microscope. Many jewelers own microscopes and encourage their customers to use it when purchasing a diamond.

When you have the necessary equipment, you can proceed as follows:

♦ **Clean the diamond**. Usually rubbing it with a lint-free cloth is sufficient. Sometimes, though, you'll need to soak it in soap and water or ethyl alcohol or even have it professionally cleaned. Avoid touching the stone with your fingers as fingers can leave smudges.

♦ **First examine the entire stone with your naked eye**. One of the criteria for assigning clarity grades is the visibility of the inclusions without magnification. Looking at the stone first with a loupe or microscope can mislead you into believing inclusions are eye visible when they aren't, because your mind has a tendency to see what it expects to see.

♦ **With a 10-power magnifier, examine the stone from various angles**—top, bottom, sides. Even though top and centrally-located inclusions are the most undesirable in terms of beauty, those seen from the sides or bottom of a stone can affect its price and durability.

♦ **Look at the stone with light shining on it from various angles**—above it, through the sides, and reflected off the surfaces. Overhead illumination will help you determine what the blemishes and inclusions look like under normal lighting conditions. Light transmitted through the sides will highlight inclusions and will usually make them more visible. Light reflected off the surface will help you identify surface cracks and blemishes.

Diamond Inclusions

Opinions differ as to how various clarity features should be classified. Some feel the term "inclusion" should be reserved for foreign matter within a stone. This book uses a broader definition, which is found in the GIA Diamond Grading Course: "**Inclusions** are characteristics which are entirely inside a stone or extend into it from the surface." The GIA defines **blemishes** as "characteristics confined to or primarily affecting the surface."

As you examine diamonds under magnification, you'll probably wonder what inclusions you're looking at. Listed below are inclusions you can find in diamonds.

♦ **Crystals** of all sorts of interesting shapes and sizes are commonly seen in diamonds (figs. 7.2 & 7.3). Over 24 different minerals have been identified as crystal inclusions in diamonds, but the most frequent type crystal seen is another diamond. Minute crystals that look like small specks under 10X magnification are called **pinpoints**. Crystals can lower the clarity grade of your diamond, but they can also turn it into a collector's item. The larger and more obvious crystals are, the more they impact the clarity grade.

With the naked eye, crystals may look like white or black spots or tiny dots. Sometimes you may hear black marks referred to as "carbon spots," but this can mislead people into believing that coal particles are in their diamonds. Eric Bruton discusses this on page 385 of his book *Diamonds* and says, "Dark inclusions in diamond were for generations called *carbon spots*, although it is now known that amorphous carbon does not occur as inclusions." More often than not, spots that look black are actually transparent.

Fig. 7.2 Black spots that are crystals and reflections of crystals

Fig. 7.3 This diamond with a garnet crystal would be appropriate for someone whose birthday is in January.

♦ **Cracks** of various sizes are also common in diamonds (figs. 7.4 to 7.7). They may also be called **fractures** or **breaks**. When they're straight and flat, they're called **cleavages**. Because of their appearance, cracks are often called **feathers**. Normally, you need not worry about cracks if they're small. The crack in figure 7.4 does not weaken the diamond and is not visible from a face-up position, so this stone still received a high grade of VS_2 (very slightly included) from the GIA. The girdle (outer edge) of diamonds often has tiny hairline cracks which are called **bearding**. Light bearding does not prevent a diamond from receiving a clarity grade of VVS (very very slightly included).

Fig. 7.4 A crack (feather) that's insignificant

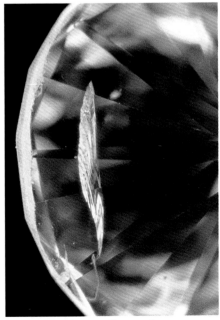

Fig. 7.5 A feather-like crack

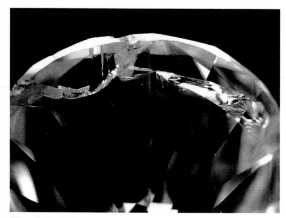

Fig. 7.6 A serious crack   **Fig. 7.7** A large, threatening crack

Larger cracks like the ones in figures 7.5 to 7.7 have a more serious effect on the clarity grade because they are more noticeable and they can sometimes threaten the stone's durability.

◆ **Clouds** are hazy or milky areas in a diamond that occasionally resemble a galaxy (fig. 7.8). Most clouds are made up of crystals too tiny to see individually under ten-power magnification. Clouds may be hard to find in diamonds with high clarity grades. When clouds are large and dense, they diminish transparency and make your diamond look undesirably white (fig. 7.9).

Fig. 7.8 A cloud near the culet of a diamond   **Fig. 7.9** A cloudy diamond with a cloud in the center

◆ **Growth or grain lines** are fine lines or ripples caused by irregular crystallization (fig. 7.10). They are also referred to as twinning lines. Sometimes diamonds look hazy or oily when many of these lines are present (fig 7.11). White, colored or reflective graining can affect the clarity grade. Colorless graining does not normally lower the clarity grade but it can sometimes affect the transparency and brilliance of a diamond. These two attributes are not included on diamond grading reports.

Fig. 7.10 Grain lines

Fig. 7.11 A grainy, hazy-looking diamond

Fig. 7.12 Large cavity on a diamond's pavilion

Fig. 7.13 Laser drill holes

♦ **Cavities** are large indentations where chunks of the diamond are missing (fig. 7.12). They may look like mountain ranges or eroded canyons.

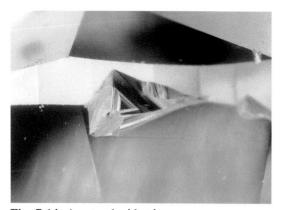

Fig. 7.14 A natural with trigons

Fig. 7.15 A natural with step-like ridges that extend onto the crown

◆ **Laser drill holes** look like suspended fishing lines (fig. 7.13). They're actually tiny holes drilled into the diamond with a laser beam, allowing black spots to be dissolved or bleached out with chemicals. This treatment is considered legitimate and normally improves the appearance. There are times, however, when the diamond looks worse after drilling due to the resulting long white drill holes. To see laser holes you usually have to tilt the diamond or view it from the side.

◆ **Knots** are included diamond crystals which are left exposed on the surface by polishing. They may look like raised areas on the diamond, and there may be a difference in polish quality between the knot and the surrounding areas when examined with reflected light.

Surface Blemishes

◆ **Scratches, nicks, pits and abraded facet edges** are not considered as serious as inclusions because they can often be polished away.

◆ **Extra facets** are additions to the normal number of facets (flat, geometric diamond surfaces). They are usually added to polish away a flaw or save diamond weight. They don't affect the clarity grade of a diamond if they are on the pavilion and can't be seen face up at ten-power magnification.

◆ **Naturals** are part of the original surface of the diamond crystal left unpolished (figs. 7.14 & 7.15). Sometimes they have step-like ridges or triangular forms (called **trigons**) on them that indicate your stone is truly a diamond. Naturals don't affect the clarity grade if they're confined to the girdle and don't distort the girdle outline.

Clarity Grading Explained

Now that we have identified diamond inclusions and blemishes, we are ready to look at how they affect clarity grades. There are various grading systems, but those that are best known resemble the one developed by the GIA (Gemological Institute of America). You can make yourself understood to any knowledgeable diamond dealer or jeweler in the world using the GIA system.

Clarity grade descriptions of all the major systems assume a trained grader working with ten-power fully corrected magnification and effective illumination. The GIA defines their clarity grades under these conditions as follows:

GIA CLARITY GRADES*	
* For trained graders using 10-power magnification and proper lighting.	
Fl	**Flawless**, no blemishes or inclusions.
IF	**Internally flawless**, no inclusions and only insignificant blemishes.
VVS₁ & VVS₂	**Very, very slightly included**, minute inclusions that are difficult to see.
VS₁ & VS₂	**Very slightly included**, minor inclusions ranging from difficult to somewhat easy to see.
SI₁ & SI₂	**Slightly included**, noticeable inclusions that are easy (SI₁) or very easy (SI₂) to see.
I₁, I₂, & I₃ In Europe: P₁, P₂ & P₃	**Imperfect**, obvious inclusions that usually are eye-visible face up; in I₃, distinctions are based on the combined effect on durability, transparency, and brilliance.

These definitions may seem unscientific, and in fact they *are* unscientific. Clarity grading is subjective and it's not always the same from lab to lab. However, trained and experienced graders usually agree on the clarity grade; untrained or inexperienced graders have more difficulty in determining clarity grades consistently. Diamonds were not created to fit into well-defined categories. Categories had to be created to differentiate already existing diamonds. This was not an easy process.

The first diamond grading system was introduced by the GIA in the late 1920's. Since then it has been debated and modified. The present system allows people throughout the world to compare and visualize degrees of clarity that are imperceptible to the naked eye.

Diamond grading is an art. That means it requires practice, and a good way of getting this practice is to start examining diamonds with the help of your jeweler. But before you look at diamonds, try forming a general mental picture of some of the clarity grades by studying the examples in figures 7.16 to 7.22. There are no photo examples of the grades from Flawless to VVS₂, because the differences don't show up well in photographs. Further details of all the categories are given in the following paragraphs:

Flawless (Fl) Flawless diamonds are rarely used in jewelry. More often than not they are kept in safes. Ordinary wear could cause them to lose their flawless status.

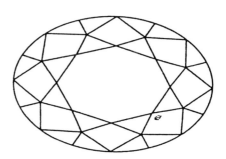

Fig. 7.16 VS₁

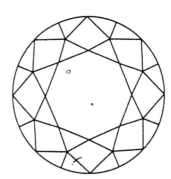

Fig. 7.17 VS₂

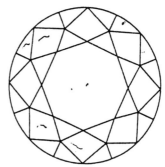

Fig. 7.18 SI₁

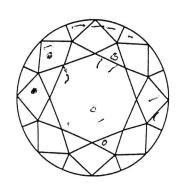

Fig. 7.19 SI₂

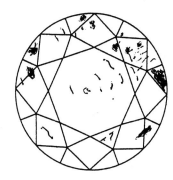

Fig. 7.20 I₁ (P₁)

Fig. 7.21 I₂ (P₂)

Fig. 7.22 I₃ (P₃)

Internally Flawless (IF) Diamonds with no inclusions and only insignificant blemishes, such as tiny pits and scratches that are easily removed with repolishing, can be classified internally flawless. It's unlikely that your jeweler has IF or Fl diamonds in stock. He might, however, be able to locate one for you.

VVS₁ & VVS₂ These diamonds have inclusions so small that the average person would not be able to find them under ten-power magnification. Even trained diamond graders may have to view the stone from several positions to find the inclusion. Some typical VVS flaws are pinpoints, minute hairline cracks, tiny bruises, bearding, and slight graining. Jewelers seldom keep VVS stones in stock, especially if they are one carat or more.

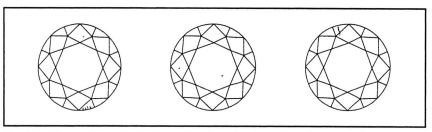

Fig. 7.23 Examples of VVS diamonds with pinpoints, bearding and minute cracks.

VS₁ A lay person would have a hard time finding the very small crystals, clouds, cracks (feathers) or pinpoints that characterize this grade. Sometimes, he may not be able to find them under ten-power magnification. Some stores keep large VS₁ diamonds in stock, but if they have a wide selection of them, be suspicious of overgrading because they're not readily available in large quantities (fig. 7.16).

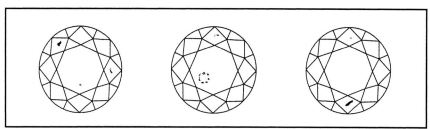

Fig. 7.24 Examples of VS₁ diamonds with small clouds, tiny cracks, and tiny crystals

VS₂ Diamonds with this classification have the same types of inclusions as VS₁ stones but the inclusions are either more numerous, larger or easier to see (fig. 7.17).

SI₁ Even though this is the seventh clarity grade from the top, this is still an excellent stone. If you look at it face-up with the unaided eye, you won't see any inclusions. If you look at it with ten-times magnification, you'll notice small cracks (feathers), clouds or crystals (fig. 7.18).

SI$_2$ Sometimes you can see the inclusions of these stones through the pavilion (bottom) of the stone with the naked eye, but normally, the inclusions are not visible through the crown (fig. 7.19). An exception to this would be with large diamonds and with emerald-cut diamonds. As the GIA points out, inclusions in such diamonds are easier to see because of their larger facets. The inclusions of the SI grades generally do not affect the durability of the stone.

SI$_3$ An intermediary grade between I$_1$ and SI$_2$, which was first introduced on reports by EGL (European Gem Lab) in Los Angeles. The GIA and AGS (American Gem Society) do not use it on their reports.

I$_1$ (P$_1$)   The inclusions of this grade are obvious at ten-power magnification, but in small brilliant-cut diamonds, they are barely visible to the unaided eye through the crown (fig. 7.20). This can be a good clarity grade choice for people on a limited budget. Often a well-cut I$_1$ looks better than a poorly cut SI diamond.

I$_2$ (P$_2$)   The inclusions are easily visible to the unaided eye and may affect the beauty and durability of the diamond (fig. 7.21). This grade is frequently used in discount jewelry.

I$_3$ (P$_3$)   These diamonds often look shattered, as if they'd been hammered. Sometimes they have no cracks, but they're so filled with crystal inclusions that they have a muddy gray or whitish look. An I$_3$ grade would be unacceptable to someone interested in a brilliant and transparent diamond.

Clarity grading requires more than identification of diamond inclusions. An overall visual impression must be formed of the diamond with and without ten-power magnification, and the grading conditions must be considered. Keep in mind the following:

◆ Each grade represents a range of quality. Consequently, diamonds of the same clarity grade are not always equally desirable. That's why its important to visually examine stones instead of just relying on grades when making your choice. In some cases, a high I$_1$ diamond can look better than a low SI$_2$ stone when set.

◆ Prongs and settings can hide flaws. Consequently, only approximate clarity grades can be assigned to diamonds set in jewelry. If you're interested in a stone with a high clarity, it may be best for you to buy a loose stone and have it set.

◆ Diamonds must be clean for accurate grading. Dirt and dust can look like inclusions.

◆ Big inclusions generally lower grades more than small ones. Usually one or two of the largest inclusions establish the clarity grade.

◆ The type of inclusion can have a dramatic effect on the grade. For example, a small crack (feather) will tend to lower a grade more than a pinpoint inclusion.

◆ Dark inclusions tend to lower grades more than colorless and white inclusions. Sometimes, however, white inclusions stand out more than black ones due to their position.

◆ Inclusions under the table (in the center) of the diamond tend to lower grades more than those near the girdle (around the edges).

Additional Clarity Examples

Fig. 7.25 A parti-colored VS$_2$ diamond

Fig. 7.26 SI$_1$

Fig. 7.27 SI$_2$

Fig. 7.28 SI$_2$

Fig. 7.29 SI$_2$

Fig. 7.30 I$_1$

Fig. 7.31 I_1

Fig. 7.32 A high I_1

♦ Your overall impression of a diamond's clarity can be affected by the diamonds it is compared to. A diamond will look better when viewed with low clarity diamonds than with high clarity ones. To have a more balanced outlook, try to look at a variety of qualities.

♦ If it's easy for you to see inclusions through the top of a diamond without magnification, it's fairly certain that the stone is an I grade.

♦ The clarity grades can also change depending on who the grader is. A one grade difference between two experienced graders is not uncommon.

♦ The higher the clarity grade of a diamond, the more it costs. Clarity differences that go unnoticed by lay people looking through a microscope can mean thousands of dollars in value in large stones of high quality. Therefore, if you are planning on investing in a large, high-clarity grade diamond, it is well worth your money to pay for an independent lab grading report on it before purchasing or insuring it. Grading reports can be expensive so they're not often done on low-clarity diamonds. Even when a grading report comes with the stone, you will probably have paid for the report indirectly, as reflected in the cost of the stone.

♦ Usually the higher the color grade of a diamond, the more the clarity grade affects its cost.

♦ Diamonds are normal, not defective, if they have inclusions.

How Lighting Can Affect Your Perception of Clarity

When professionals use microscopes to judge clarity, they normally examine the stones with a lighting set up called **darkfield illumination.** This is a diffused lighting which comes up diagonally through the bottom of the gemstone. (A frosted or shaded bulb provides **diffused** light, a clear bulb does not.) In this lighting, tiny inclusions and even dust particles will stand out in high relief. As a result, the clarity of the stone appears worse than it would under normal conditions (figures 7.4 & 7.36 provide examples of this).

When looking at jewelry with the unaided eye, you normally view it with **overhead lighting.** This lighting is above the stone (not literally over a person's head). Overhead lighting is reflected off the facets, whereas darkfield lighting is transmitted through the stone. If you ask salespeople to show you a diamond under a microscope, it's unlikely that they'll use its overhead lamp. Instead they may only have you view the stone under darkfield illumination. The inclusions will look more prominent than under overhead lights. To get a balanced perspective of the stone, also look at the diamond with a loupe and light above the stone.

How Lighting, Magnification, Positioning and Focus Affect Clarity

Fig. 7.34 Same diamond at 10x magnification viewed with darkfield lighting, which highlights inclusions. The only way to bring the major inclusions all into focus was to tilt the diamond at an angle. If the stone were face up, they wouldn't all be clearly visible.

The main inclusions are: top left, a crack (feather); top right, some tiny crystals with stress fractures; and bottom center, a colorless crystal. SI$_1$-size inclusions like these don't affect the beauty or durability of a stone and they can help prove a diamond is genuine and natural.

Fig. 7.33 A 6.6mm diamond, photographed face-up through a microscope with overhead lighting and magnified 10 times. Only a crack (feather) at the 12 o'clock position is easily visible. It has an AGS lab report stating its clarity grade is SI$_1$ and its cut grade is AGS Ideal 0, their highest cut grade.

Fig 7.35 Approximate actual size of the diamond in figures 7.33 & 7.34. When viewed without magnification, the inclusions are not visible. This is a beautiful diamond despite the fact that it has microscopic "flaws," which distinguish it from all other diamonds. In this view, the author photographed the diamond with a camera macro lens.

Fig. 7.36 Top part of the same diamond magnified about 25 times and viewed with darkfield illumination.

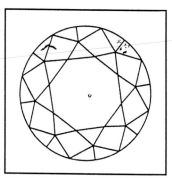

Fig. 7.37 Diagram of the major inclusions in figure 7.34

Besides making flaws more prominent, darkfield illumination hides brilliance. To accurately assess the beauty, brilliance and transparency of a diamond, you should view it with overhead lighting. The quickest and easiest way to see a diamond's beauty magnified is with a good 10-power loupe. Most of the loose diamonds in this book were taken with overhead lighting or a combination of transmitted and overhead lighting.

Judging Transparency

If you saw an ad saying "One-carat diamonds—Just $999," you'd probably wonder how a store could sell them at such a low price. It's quite possible they have poor transparency. Their prices are low because cloudy or murky diamonds lack brilliance and are hard to sell. Diamonds are supposed to be transparent.

Transparency is defined in the *GIA Diamond Dictionary* as the: "degree to which a material transmits light without appreciable scattering, so that objects beyond are entirely visible." In other words, transparency refers to how clear, hazy, cloudy or opaque a material is.

Clarity and transparency are interconnected but they're different. If there's a cloudy spot in a transparent diamond, the cloud is a clarity feature. If the entire diamond is cloudy due to submicroscopic inclusions, then the cloudiness is a matter of transparency. However, this should affect the clarity grade of the diamond.

In most cases, clarity grades won't help you select transparent diamonds. This is because:
♦ Clarity grades don't normally take into account subtle differences in transparency.
♦ Diamonds with obvious transparency problems are rarely submitted to labs for grading. More often than not they're mounted in bargain-priced jewelry.
♦ When translucent and semi-translucent diamonds are sent to labs for grading, the clarity grades are usually omitted at the request of the dealers paying for the reports. The stones could, however, receive a an impressive-sounding color grade of "fancy white."

If you'd like to buy a brilliant diamond, select one with good transparency. This is not hard for a lay person to do. Just look at the diamond through the sides and check if it's as clear as crystal glass or distilled water. Face-up it should be brilliant and there should be a strong contrast between the dark and bright areas. A well-cut diamond should not have a see-through effect.

When judging transparency, make sure the diamond is clean; examine it both with your naked eye and a 10-power magnifier, and look at it under different lighting conditions (fluorescent light, incandescent light, sunlight, and away from light). Keep in mind that white objects or walls can reflect into the diamond making it appear less transparent than it really is.

It's helpful to have a transparent diamond sample for comparison. Nuances of transparency and haziness are more easily detected, and your evaluation will be more accurate.

You won't need a comparison stone or magnification to spot diamonds with serious transparency problems. You can see their cloudiness from several feet away. If the diamonds don't sparkle and shine even under the store's special spotlights, then there's definitely a problem. The diamonds will probably look worse away from the lights.

Dirty diamonds resemble low-grade milky diamonds. Therefore, after you receive or purchase diamond jewelry, clean it regularly; you'll be able to appreciate more the brilliance and beauty of your diamonds.

Transparency Examples

Fig. 7.38 A diamond with high transparency

Fig. 7.39 A cloudy diamond

Fig. 7.40 A slightly hazy diamond

Fig. 7.41 A diamond with graining that gives it an oily appearance

Fig. 7.42 A low-grade diamond with inadequate transparency. As a result, the cutter wasn't motivated to proportion it well. It has a deep pavilion, as evidenced by the dark center. In addition, the crown is too shallow.

Fig. 7.43 Another low-grade diamond with inadequate transparency. This one has strong bearding (fringed edge).

If you have some milky white diamonds, you can put them to good use by mounting them with fancy-color diamonds and creating a design or picture with them. You can also use them as a starting point for a collection of diamonds of different colors.

Why Transparency is Listed as a Separate Price Factor in This Book

When the concept of the 4 C's was developed, non-transparent diamond rough was used for industrial purposes; it wasn't faceted into gemstones. The issue of transparency was irrelevant because diamonds sold in jewelry stores were generally all transparent.

Times have changed. Recently, I discovered that two people who'd read the fifth edition of my diamond book ended up getting cloudy diamonds from respectable jewelry stores. Given this situation, I realized I hadn't adequately dealt with the subject of transparency. I should have presented it as a separate value factor so their attention would have been more focused on getting a diamond with good transparency.

Other people have also addressed the issue of diamond transparency. One example is Eddy Vleeschadrager, a noted author, diamond dealer and cutter. In his book *Dureté 10, Le diamant (Hardness 10, Diamond)*, he says:

The degree of diamond transparency can vary enormously, from the greatest limpidity to the strongest opacity. Regarding jewelry diamonds, the most transparent are called "gems."
Some stones have opaque areas resembling a milky white cloud. They're not cut because if the cloud is at the heart of the stone, they won't have any brilliance after cutting. These are called "dead stones" (translation of Section 10 on page 65).

Even though many cutters would never facet milky-white rough into diamonds, some will do so if their customers are looking for cheap, promotional merchandise or if they sell stones to collectors. Collectors sometimes describe milky diamonds as "opalescent." On page 254 of his book *Collecting and Classifying Coloured Diamonds*, 254, Steve Hofer, a gemologist, cutter and president of Colored Diamond Laboratory Services, states:

An opalescent diamond correctly refers to white diamonds with a milky or cloudy appearance, typical of the milky or cloudy appearance of common opal. In this instance, the term opalescent has nothing to do with the flashes of color seen in precious opal, which result from diffraction of light.

Since low grade cloudy diamonds are becoming more prevalent, and since some of the terms used to identify them are misleading, I've concluded that transparency should be listed as a separate value factor. Here are some other reasons for treating it as a distinct factor:

♦ Consumers are often told "the whiter the diamond the better." If they interpret this statement literally, they may think milky white diamonds are desirable and valuable, when in fact they aren't. This confusion won't occur if they learn how transparency affects value. To avoid confusion, this book describes D, E & F color diamonds as colorless rather than white. The less color a diamond has, the greater its value, with the exception of fancy color diamonds.

♦ When transparency is treated as a separate factor, you learn the importance of examining diamonds visually, instead of just relying on lab reports and grades. There are no grades on lab reports that measure diamond transparency, even though it has a major impact on value. In addition, most diamond jewelry is not sold with lab reports.

If you're buying a semi-mount, tennis bracelet or brooch, you'll need to be able to make a global assessment of the diamonds and determine if they have "life." In other words, are the diamonds transparent and brilliant? These are key factors in evaluating mounted diamonds. No matter how well cut diamonds are, if they don't have good transparency, their brilliance will be seriously diminished.

◆ Transparency is already considered a separate factor in colored stone evaluation. AGL (The American Gemological Laboratories) even includes it as a factor on their lab reports, but they call it "texture." Transparency is just as important for diamonds as it is for colored gems.

◆ Some people in the trade have incorrectly linked transparency to UV fluorescence (a glow under ultraviolet light; see Chapter 5). You may read on the Internet or in literature statements such as:

"If a diamond has fluorescence, it will have a cloudy or milky appearance, especially in sunlight."

"Two out of every three diamonds have fluorescence that causes the diamond to look oily and milky in sunlight."

People would realize these statements were false if they were taught to judge diamond transparency as a separate value factor. They'd be able to look at transparent, fluorescent, diamonds under different lighting and see their transparency. Just because a few fluorescent diamonds have a hazy, oily or cloudy appearance, doesn't mean they all do. Non-fluorescent diamonds can also look hazy or cloudy. Judge transparency with your eyes instead of by reading a fluorescence comment on a lab report.

You can get more information on this subject in the Winter 1997 issue of *Gems & Gemology* in the article entitled "A Contribution to Understanding the Effect of Blue Fluorescence on the Appearance of Diamonds." The GIA didn't find a correlation between diamond fluorescence and transparency. Blue fluorescence can, however, affect your perception of diamond color by making yellowish diamonds appear less yellow.

No one knows exactly what percentage of the world's diamonds are fluorescent because nobody has access to all of the world's diamonds. In addition, estimates based on statistical sampling vary according to how one defines "non-fluorescent."

Tom Tashey, who has directed diamond grading at the GIA, EGL and now PGS (Professional Gem Sciences), believes that when "inert" and "none" are used to describe a diamond's fluorescence, it should mean there is absolutely no visible fluorescence. Based on this definition he estimates that only 2 to 3% of all the diamonds he's graded at the GIA, EGL and PGS have been non-fluorescent. In other words, 97 to 98% of the diamonds he's graded have had at least a very faint degree of fluorescence. Tashey further estimates that 25 to 35% of the diamonds he's graded have had a medium to strong fluorescence. And of all the hundreds of thousands of diamonds he's examined, only about 10–12 of the fluorescent stones had an oily or cloudy transparency. Dealers don't normally send cloudy diamonds to labs for grading.

If you own a diamond accompanied by a lab report with a fluorescence description of "none" or "inert," this doesn't necessarily mean the diamond is non-fluorescent. It just means that according to that lab's standards, the diamond didn't display enough fluorescence to be considered fluorescent.

Blue fluorescence does not have a negative impact on a diamond's beauty. However, inadequate transparency usually does. This is one of the main reasons why fluorescence and transparency should be treated as separate factors when evaluating and identifying diamonds.

8

Diamond or Imitation?

Anyone can be fooled by imitations (also called **simulants**), even diamond experts. However, by doing the following tests, you can reduce your chances of being fooled.

See-through Test

Look at the stone face up. Can you see through it? If you can, it's probably an imitation (In some cases a poor cut or the presence of dirt or grease makes it possible to see through a diamond). The see-through test can also be done by placing a clean, round stone face down on newsprint (fig 8.1). If you can see the letters through the stone, it probably is an imitation. For fancy shapes such as ovals and pears, it's best to limit this test to the face-up view because often, you can see through their pavilions.

If you plan to examine stones in antique jewelry, you should be aware that the diamonds may have a see-through effect due to the different cut and the large culet.

Tilt Test

Tilt the stone against a dark background. Can you see an obvious, dark, fan-shaped area (fig. 8.2)? If you can, it's doubtful that it is a diamond. This test is a variation of the see-through test, but it's easier to do on mounted stones. It also works best on round diamonds. Poorly proportioned fancy-shape diamonds may also display a dark fan-shaped area.

Fig. 8.1 See-through test. Note how the print cannot be seen through the diamond in the lower center. To the top left is a synthetic spinel and to the top right, is a cubic zirconia.

Fig. 8.2 Tilt test. Note the black fan-shaped area of the synthetic spinel to the right of the diamond.

Fig. 8.3 You can see the mounting through the V-shaped area which forms as this cubic zirconia is tilted.

Fig. 8.4 A see-through effect and pale rainbow colors are visible in this mounted cubic zirconia. *Photo and ring from Varna Platinum.*

Rainbow Colors Test Move the stone under a light and note how strong the flashes of rainbow colors are in comparison to a diamond under the same light. If the rainbow colors (also called **dispersion** or **fire**) are a lot more obvious than your diamond, the stone may be synthetic rutile, strontium titanate or synthetic moissanite. If they're less obvious, the stone may be another imitation or a diamond with a large table and a thin crown. This test is most useful for distinguishing diamond from synthetic rutile, strontium titanate and synthetic moissanite, the three imitations which, like diamond, can be cut to have no see-through effect.

CZ (cubic zirconia) also displays more rainbow colors than diamond, but sometimes it's hard for the untrained eye to see the difference. It's particularly important to compare CZ and diamond under the same light. The rainbow colors are easier to see in sunlight and under incandescent light (from light bulbs) than under fluorescent light.

Closed-back Test If the stone is set in jewelry, look at the back of the setting. Is the pavilion (bottom) of the stone blocked from view or enclosed in metal (fig. 8.5)? Normally, the bottom of a diamond is at least partially visible (fig. 8.6). Therefore, if you can only see the crown or top of the stone, you need to investigate carefully.

An open-back setting does not indicate that a stone is a diamond. Imitation diamonds are often set with the pavilion showing. But a completely closed back is often a sign that something is being hidden. Maybe the stone is a rhinestone (glass with a foil back). Maybe the stone is a diamond with a coating to improve its color. Maybe the stone is a single-cut diamond made to appear like a more expensive brilliant-cut diamond. No matter what might be hidden, to avoid being duped, it is best to buy a diamond in a setting with part of the pavilion showing if you're not dealing with someone you know and trust.

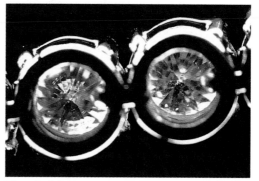

Fig. 8.5 Glass stones in closed-back settings   **Fig. 8.6** Diamonds in open-back settings

If you have antique jewelry, you should not assume that foil-backed stones in enclosed settings are rhinestones. Prior to the eighteenth century, it was common practice to put a foil backing on diamonds to improve their brilliance.

Recently, some jewelry manufacturers have used solid backs under their channel-set diamonds to increase the rigidity of the channel mountings. This allows the diamonds to be set more securely. In most cases, however, it is still customary to set diamonds with part of the pavilion showing.

Price Test   Is the stone being sold at an unbelievably low price? If it is, it might be an imitation or stolen or defective merchandise. Jewelers have to pay a lot for diamonds, and they cannot stay in business if they sell their diamonds below their cost.

Thermal Conduction Test

GIA GEM Pocket Diamond Tester with warning buzzer

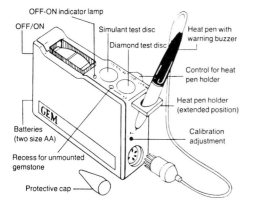

OFF-ON indicator lamp
OFF/ON
Simulant test disc
Diamond test disc
Heat pen with warning buzzer
Control for heat pen holder
Heat pen holder (extended position)
Batteries (two size AA)
Calibration adjustment
Recess for unmounted gemstone
Protective cap

Fig. 8.7. *Diagram courtesy GIA*

An easy, quick and accurate way of determining if a stone is a diamond imitation is to test it with an instrument like the GIA GEM pocket thermal tester (fig 8.7), which measures the heat conductivity of the stone. A metal probe or heat pen is pressed on a facet of the stone. Then the needle of the instrument's meter reads *diamond* or *imitation*.

Before 1998, the thermal conduction test could detect all commercial diamond simulants. Then, a new imitation was introduced to the market—**synthetic moissanite**, chemically known as silicon carbide. It reacts like diamond to the thermal conduction test, but there are other ways to help identify it, (e.g.; doubled facet test, specific gravity, reflectivity, moissanite tester). Moissanite retails for several hundred dollars per carat, making it the highest priced diamond imitation.

The pocket tester in figure 8.7 can be purchased from the GIA Gem Instruments Corporation in New York City or in Carlsbad, California.

Fig. 8.8 Natural with trigons on a diamond girdle

Fig. 8.9 Natural with ridges on a diamond girdle

Fig. 8.10 Note the lines and the angular shape of the natural on this diamond girdle.

Fig. 8.11 A distinctly different rounded formation is visible on the girdle of this cubic zirconia.

Girdle Test

With a 10-power magnifier, examine the girdle (the narrow band around the outer edge of the stone). If the girdle has been carefully formed and/or faceted, it's most likely a diamond or possibly a synthetic moissanite. It's not financially feasible for the manufacturers of other imitation diamonds to put high-quality girdles on their stones. An individual whose goal is to deceive could, however, cut any imitation with a diamond-like girdle.

Many diamonds have poorly-made girdles that resemble those of imitation stones. But they may have **naturals** (portions of the original surface of the rough diamond), which distinguish them from simulants. The girdles of imitation stones may also have formations that can be mistaken for naturals. But these tend to be rounded unlike diamond naturals which are usually angular and may have step-like ridges, lines or **trigons** (triangular indented growth marks).

Doubled Facet Test

This is a key test for detecting synthetic moissanite. If you see doubled facets or a doubled table reflection when you look at the stone through a magnifier, then the stone is not a diamond. Diamond refracts light in a single direction, so its facets appear as single lines. Synthetic moissanite and synthetic rutile are doubly refractive and display doubling. Synthetic rutile diamond simulants, however, can easily be detected with a thermal diamond tester. To detect doubling, you normally need to tilt the stone and look at it from an angle. Defocusing the microscope or focusing at a point past the culet will also make doubling more apparent.

Fig. 8.12 Gas bubbles, concave facets, rounded facet edges, uneven surfaces, swirly lines and formations are all visible in these glass diamond imitations. Glass stones do not always show these characteristics.

Glass Test

Colorless glass is often used to imitate diamond. Some of the characteristics of glass are as follows:

♦ Gas bubbles. In glass they are round, oval, elongated or shaped like donuts. Gas bubbles may also be visible in other imitations.

♦ Obviously rounded facet edges. Real diamonds of good quality normally have sharp, well-defined facet edges and junctions. Other imitations such as synthetic moissanite may also have rounded facet edges, but the rounding is not as obvious as on glass imitations.

♦ Concave facets and surfaces

♦ Swirly lines or formations

♦ Uneven or pitted surfaces. Pits may be found on other imitations too.

The best way to learn to recognize glass is to start looking at it closely. Look at some inexpensive drinking glasses with a loupe. There will probably be some bubbles and often they will be visible with the naked eye. Large bubbles are one of the most reliable indications of glass. Look at cheap costume jewelry with a loupe whenever you get a chance and try to find the above characteristics. The more you examine glass, the better you will become at identifying it.

There are other tests for distinguishing diamonds from imitations, but many of them require special training or equipment. Nevertheless, you may be curious about how gemologists identify diamonds. Therefore, other methods have been listed below.

♦ The interior and exterior of the stone are examined under magnification. Diamonds can have special characteristics such as included diamond crystals, distinctive graining, laser drill holes, naturals and trigons. Imitations are often flawless or have gas bubbles. Synthetic moissanite may have whitish needles, surface pits, polish lines and/or rounded facets and facet junctions. If chips or fractures are present, they'll have curved, conchoidal surfaces (fig. 8.16).

♦ The stone is examined for transparency. Diamonds are noted for their high transparency, so if it looks hazy, it might be an imitation like cubic zirconia. There are, however, many hazy and cloudy diamonds. Consequently, several other tests should be applied before concluding the stone is an imitation.

91

Some Characteristics of Synthetic Moissanite

Fig. 8.13 Doubling of the facet edges and the table reflection, which become visible as the stone is tilted or as the microscope is defocused

Fig. 8.14 Spectral colors which are stronger than those of diamond and cubic zirconia

Fig. 8.15 Facet edges and junctions which are a little more rounded than those of diamonds

Fig. 8.16 Conchoidal (shell-shaped) fractures and chips

Fig. 8.17 Girdles such as this faceted one, which may resemble those of diamond or quickly cut girdles which look like those of low-priced imitations

Fig. 8.18 A brilliance resembling that of diamond. Face-up view of the moissanite stone in figures 8.13 to 8.17.

◆ The reflective capacity of the stone can be measured with an instrument called a reflectometer. Diamond and its simulants have characteristic readings. It's crucial that the stone be very clean and polished, otherwise you may get misleading readings. One type of reflectometer is called the "Diamond Eye" and is made by Hanneman Gemological Instruments in Poulsbo, WA.

◆ The weight of the stone can be compared to the weight of diamonds of the same size. With the exception of glass, diamonds generally weigh less than imitations of the same size. In other words diamonds have a lower specific gravity (3.52) than most imitations. This means the diamonds will sink more slowly in heavy liquids than most simulants.

One important exception is synthetic moissanite, which has a lower specific gravity than diamond (3.22). A quick and easy way to separate loose diamonds from synthetic moissanites is to place them in methylene iodide (a heavy liquid, S.G. 3.32). Synthetic moissanites will float whereas the diamonds will sink. Methylene iodide is very toxic and should only be used in a very well ventilated room.

◆ The stone is x-rayed. Diamonds are extremely transparent to x-rays. Imitations aren't. Diamonds also normally fluoresce blue when exposed to x-rays.

◆ A light is directed through the stone and viewed with an instrument called a spectroscope to measure how it absorbs light. Diamonds have characteristic readings.

◆ The stone is placed under short-wave and long-wave ultraviolet light and the fluorescence is compared to that of a diamond.

◆ A moissanite testing instrument is used after the stones are tested with a thermal diamond tester. It quickly distinguishes diamonds from synthetic moissanites. One type of moissanite tester is made by C3, the company that produces and markets synthetic moissanite. It works by recognizing the absorption or reflection of the near-ultraviolet portion of the spectrum. It's available from C3 in Morrisville, NC or Rio Grande in Albuquerque, NM. The C3 tester gives correct results for moissanites and colorless to near colorless diamonds. Some fancy color diamonds, however, elicit misleading reactions with the C3 tester.

Perhaps you've heard of hardness tests in which the stone is scratched with something like a carbide scriber. If the stone can't be scratched, it is assumed to be a diamond because of its exceptional hardness. Most diamond professionals would advise against using this test because of the risk of damage to the stone. It's not a necessary test and the results can be misleading. The following story illustrates this.

Several years ago, a pawnbroker in the USA was called to a bank by a government official and relative of a deceased person. They wanted him to examine a large colorless emerald-cut stone in the safe-deposit box of the deceased person and verify if it was a diamond. After a quick look with his loupe, the pawnbroker said it was definitely not a diamond. The official and relative asked the pawnbroker to explain why he thought it was an imitation because it seemed odd to put a worthless stone in a safe. He indicated that it was too good to be a diamond; and to further prove his claim, the pawnbroker took a diamond hardness point tool out of his briefcase. Pressing hard, he scratched three deep x's on the table of the stone while contending that real diamonds can't be scratched. Later on, a GIA certificate was found identifying the stone as a D flawless diamond. Needless to say, the pawnbroker was sued.

Despite the fact that diamond is the hardest substance known to man, it can be chipped and cracked by non-diamond objects. If you have any doubt, ask a professional diamond setter. He has to always be on guard against damaging diamonds with setting tools. Hardness and toughness are not the same. Hardness is a material's resistance to scratching and abrasions. Toughness is a material's resistance to breakage, chipping and cracking. Even though diamond is the hardest gem, it's not the toughest. Because of its internal structure, diamond can chip and break easier than materials like jade.

While reading this chapter, some people may understandably ask, "Why should anyone spend so much money on a diamond when so many tests are required to distinguish it from an imitation?" This is like asking, "Why should anyone buy the painting of a well-known artist when reproductions are available for so much less?" One of the main reasons is that it can be a pleasure to own the real thing. Also, significant differences do exist between diamonds and the stones that imitate them. Often, it's easy for even a lay person to see these differences. This chapter, however, had to take into consideration the cases when the differences are not readily visible.

Some people may also be asking "Why was it necessary to create diamond imitations like CZ." To them, imitation stones may just be objects of deception, and the process of stone identification may be an undesirable chore. In actuality, identifying stones can be fun and challenging. It's like being a detective.

It's true that imitation diamonds may be used to deceive people, but they also have a positive side. Some of the reasons we should be glad they exist are:

◆ Imitations allow a person who can't afford diamonds to own stones that resemble them.

◆ Because of diamond imitations, there is a greater variety of costume jewelry. Even people who can afford diamonds and gold appreciate having an alternative to diamond jewelry when they travel or walk around high risk areas.

◆ Diamond imitations indirectly contribute to keeping real diamond jewelry costs down. Jewelers and jewelry manufacturers can display and promote their jewelry using samples set with imitation stones. This lowers their insurance and liability exposure, a cost which would otherwise have to be passed on to the consumer.

◆ Diamond imitations can also give us an appreciation for the real stone. When good diamonds are compared side by side with imitations, it is much easier to notice the high brilliance and incredible transparency that only a diamond can have.

The more time you spend identifying and comparing diamonds to imitations, the faster you will become at noting the differences between them and the harder it will be for people to deceive you. You will appreciate the diamonds you already own much more, and you'll be better qualified to spot good value as you shop for new diamonds.

9

Diamond Treatments

When the first edition of the *Diamond Ring Buying Guide* was published in 1989, there was no chapter on treatments because it wasn't an important topic. Even though some diamonds were laser drilled so black flaws could be bleached away, the drill holes were obvious under 10-power magnification. A few diamonds had coated surfaces to mask their yellow color, but this was considered an unethical trade practice; no legitimate jeweler sold such diamonds. Diamonds colored by irradiation represented only a tiny fraction of the diamonds sold on the market.

The Fifth Edition of the *Diamond Ring Buying Guide* in 1996 had a chapter entitled "Fracture-filled Diamonds." It was a hot topic because these diamonds began appearing on the market in substantial quantities in the 1990's. The fracture filling process, however, had been developed in 1982 by Israeli inventor Zvi Yehuda. The Yehuda treatment is a way of improving diamond clarity by filling narrow cracks with a thin film of molten glass.

In 1999, jewelry trade magazines announced that General Electric was able to turn a special class of brown diamonds colorless by heating them with high pressure and high temperature (HPHT treatment). Brown diamonds typically sell for about 40% to 75% less than colorless diamonds of the same quality and size. By the end of 1999, some of these HPHT-treated diamonds were being sold under the names of Pegasus, GE-POL, Monarch or the generic name "processed diamond." In 2000, a new brand name for them was introduced—"Bellataire."

Curiously, HPHT-treated diamonds are being sold in upscale stores. Even though jewelers buy them at about 15% less than untreated stones, some are able to sell them to customers at a premium by emphasizing their rarity. The customers are not told that jewelers won't pay a premium for heat-treated diamonds and that these diamonds will become more common.

At a Tucson Seminar in 2001, Branko Deljanin and Greg Sherman of the European Gem Laboratory in New York City reported that other companies were changing or lightening diamond color by the HPHT process and that the changes were not limited to one class of brown diamonds.

New ways of lasering diamonds have also been developed. Laser drilling is no longer as obvious as it once was. Consequently disclosure is more important.

When the concept of the 4 C's was conceived, diamond treatments were not an issue. That is changing as more and more treatments are being developed. It's no longer sufficient to ask what the color and clarity of a diamond is. You need to know if the color and clarity are natural or the result of a treatment. Treatment status can have a significant impact on value. Unlike colored gems, the majority of diamonds sold in stores are still untreated. You just can no longer assume that they're not treated. Verify that diamonds are untreated by asking.

Fig. 9.1 Before and after views of a fracture-filled diamond. *Photo courtesy of the Yehuda Diamond Co.*

Fracture Filling

Fracture filling is a method of improving clarity and transparency by filling cracks with a substance that makes them almost invisible. The cracks which are filled in diamonds are not large gaps; they're extremely narrow. The filler used is a glass-like thin film, so the filling process does not add measurable weight to the stone. Even though you may not see them, the filled cracks are still present in the diamond. Two other names for the diamond filling process are **glass infilling** and **clarity enhancement**.

The main advantage of the fracture-filled diamonds is cost. A stone that looks like it's worth $2000, may sell for only $1500. That's because the purchase price of the diamond before treatment was based on its unfilled appearance. In addition, the companies that process the stones have encouraged jewelers to pass on the savings to consumers. A major disadvantage of this treatment is that it's not always permanent.

The GIA Gem Trade laboratory did an extensive study of fracture-filled diamonds from three of the chief commercial sources—Yehuda/Diascience, Koss & Shechter/Genesis II and Goldman Oved/Clarity Enhanced Diamond House. The results were published in the Fall 1994 issue of *Gems & Gemology*. Regarding the durability of diamond fillings, the GIA scientists concluded that "prolonged exposure—or numerous short exposures—to commonly employed cleaning methods may sometimes damage filling substances." They also found that "repolishing or jewelry repair procedures involving direct exposure to heat (as in retipping prongs) will damage and partially remove the filler from such treated diamonds." However, "jewelry repair procedures involving indirect heating (as in sizing a ring) might not damage the fillings." In addition, extended exposure to the ultraviolet radiation of sunlight might cause fillings containing bromine to cloud and discolor. The Yehuda-treated diamonds tested by the GIA did not show any changes when exposed to ultraviolet radiation.

Prior to the GIA report, Sharon Wakefield, a gemologist-appraiser in Idaho, had conducted a study of six Koss-filled diamonds. She also concluded that these fracture-filled diamonds can be adversely affected by direct heat and cumulative exposure to cleaning procedures or the sun's ultraviolet radiation. (This was reported in the Autumn 1993 issue of *Cornerstone*, "Fracture-Filled Diamonds: A Ticking Time Bomb?")

Many of the jewelers who sell fracture-filled stones as an affordable alternative to untreated diamonds inform their customers about the treatment and its durability problems. Unfortunately, not everyone does. The three treatment firms mentioned above have publicly urged sellers to disclose fracture-filled diamonds.

Some of the stores that disclose fracture-filled diamonds do it in a misleading way. They may stamp "Clarity Enhanced" on the invoice but neglect to explain and mention the fracture filling process during the sales presentation. Most consumers don't know that a **clarity enhanced diamond** is one that's been treated to improve its clarity. What's more, some consumers think clarity enhanced stones must be better and more valuable than untreated stones, which is false. Customers should be forewarned that direct heat, acid, repolishing or repeated cleaning procedures may remove or damage the fillers. Not all sellers do this.

Detecting Fracture Fillings

Fracture-filled diamonds can be detected by using a binocular microscope along with a variety of illumination techniques. Three of the most common features seen in these diamonds are:

♦ **Color flashes**. Fracture-filled diamonds display flashes of color in their filled areas as the stones are rotated or rocked. Yehuda-treated diamonds of the 80's showed an orangy flash that changed to blue when the background of the break became bright (fig. 9.5). The fillings in the more recent Yehuda stones flash violet to purple to pink against a black background (fig. 9.2) and green to yellow against white (fig. 9.3). Similar colors were seen in the Koss- and Goldman Oved-treated stones but the colors tended to be either less saturated or more subtle.

Don't confuse the flash effects of filled diamonds with the flashes of blue and orange seen off the facets of untreated diamonds. These normal color flashes appear as patches of color rather than as the outline of a fracture or drill-hole.

♦ **Trapped bubbles in the filling**. Most filled stones show some bubbles. Sometimes they look like tiny pinpoints and in other cases they may be fairly large. Figures 9.2 and 9.5 show examples of these bubbles.

♦ **Cloudy filled areas**. Glass infilled stones may show "white clouds" in part of the filling. Some of these clouds may be groups of minute bubbles.

Filled stones can often be detected with just a 10-power loupe. For example, the colored fracture flashes of the diamond in figures 9.2 to 9.4 are easy for a lay person to see with a normal loupe or even a 5-power hand magnifier. No special lighting other than a lamp is needed. The stone has several filled fractures so the moment you look at it from the bottom, you see the flashes. Normally, however, stones must be rotated, rocked and viewed from several angles. It's especially important to view the pavilion of the stone from the bottom and the sides. Loupes with built-in lights (darkfield loupes) can be helpful.

Unfortunately, not all filled diamonds are easy to detect with a loupe. The flash effects of stones with small cracks, thick fillings or subtle flashes may be hard to see with a loupe and may require microscopic examination along with special lighting techniques such as fiber-optic illumination. Mounted stones, in particular, can pose problems because the viewing angles and visibility are restricted.

Another complication is the fact that fractures in untreated diamonds can also display colors. These normally consist of a sequence of rainbow-like colors (fig. 9.6), but sometimes only one or two colors can be seen. Typically, unfilled cracks have a feathery appearance unlike filled cracks, but this is easiest to see with the high-power magnification of a microscope. The viewing

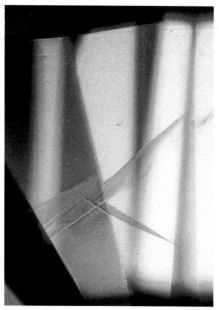

Fig. 9.2 Pink and red flash effect colors along with tiny bubbles in a Yehuda-treated diamond

Fig. 9.3 The color flashes become turquoise when the same stone is angled to make the background brightly lit.

Fig. 9.4 Face-up view of the diamond in figures 9.2 and 9.3

Fig. 9.5 Note the bluish color and bubbles in the fracture of this diamond with an earlier Yehuda filling.

Fig 9.6 Note the iridescent colors and feathery appearance of this unfilled crack.

angle is important when determining if a crack is filled or not. As the GIA points out, "Iridescent colors in unfilled breaks are usually best seen at a viewing angle roughly perpendicular to the break, whereas flash effects in filled breaks are usually detected when looking almost parallel (edge-on) to the break."

A loupe can be very helpful in spotting many fillings, but as GIA researchers have stated, *a 10x loupe cannot be relied on to detect characteristic features in all filled diamonds. Instead a binocular microscope with a range of lighting options should be used.* More detailed information on filling detection is provided in the fall 1994 and summer 1995 editions of *Gems & Gemology*. They can be ordered by calling the GIA at (800) 421-7250, ext. 7142.

Laser Drilling

Laser drilling is another type of clarity enhancement. Its purpose is to get rid of dark inclusions. A focused laser beam is used to drill a narrow hole to the dark area in the diamond. If the inclusion is not vaporized by the laser itself, then it's dissolved or bleached with acid. After the treatment, the hole looks like a white dot face-up and like a thin white line from the side-view of the stone (fig. 9.7). If the hole is filled, it can be as hard to spot as a filled fracture. Such a stone is considered to be both filled and drilled.

The summer 2000 issue of *Gems & Gemology* reported a new type of laser treatment, which typically does not have a surface reaching drill hole. The lasering causes small cleavages (flat cracks) to develop or expand around black inclusions located near the surface. Bleach can then be introduced into any cleavage reaching the surface. It's harder to detect this lasering treatment because the cleavages resemble natural inclusions instead of being obvious drill holes.

Lasering is an older and more accepted form of treatment than fracture filling, irradiation, and HPHT treatment. Many dealers will sell lasered diamonds even though they may refuse to carry other types of treated diamonds in their inventory. The reasons for this are:

♦ Laser drilling is a permanent treatment. The dark spots won't reappear later on and lower the clarity grade of the stone. Fracture filling, on the other hand, is reversible. A filled stone that looks good today might appear quite flawed sometime in the future. Some irradiated diamonds can change color if they come in contact with a jeweler's torch. Coatings can wear away.

♦ Laser drilling only affects the drilled area of the diamond; it doesn't alter the overall internal character of the diamond the way high temperature heat treatment does.

Fig. 9.7 Laser drill holes in a diamond   **Fig. 9.8** Same diamond viewed face-up

◆ Laser drilling does not add a foreign substance to the diamond. It only removes black inclusions. To many dealers, diamonds with cracks lined with glass-like fillings aren't completely natural.

◆ Laser-drilled diamonds are just as durable as untreated diamonds. They aren't damaged by normal cleaning and repair procedures. Fracture fillings and coatings may be removed, clouded or discolored when diamonds are recut, repolished, repeatedly cleaned, or when exposed to the high heat of a jeweler's torch. High temperature heat treatment can make some stones brittle and more susceptible to abrasions and chipping.

All treatments are supposed to be disclosed to consumers, whether they're accepted or not. It's not enough, though, to know if a stone has been clarity enhanced. You must also know how it's been enhanced and how you should care for it.

Coatings

Diamonds are occasionally coated to improve their color grade. A flouride coating such as that applied to lenses masks the diamond's yellow body color. Usually the coating is applied to the pavilion (bottom), but occasionally it's applied thinly only at or near the girdle. Diamonds have also been coated with colored nail polish, enamel and other substances. Sometimes a tiny amount of blue ink is applied to the girdle under the prongs to improve the apparent color.

Since coatings on diamonds are not permanent, they're not an accepted form of treatment. Coating is usually a deceptive trade practice, and is therefore not disclosed. It's detected with magnification, solvents and color filters. However, detection can be difficult. You can avoid buying coated diamonds by dealing with reputable jewelers and by getting a lab report or appraisal from qualified professionals.

Irradiation + Heating

Light yellow and brown diamonds are sometimes irradiated to produce green, blue, yellow, orange, black (very dark green) and occasionally pink, purple, or red-colored diamonds. Usually the treatment is followed by heating at about 800°–1000°C to improve the irradiated colors, which are often very dark. The color of irradiated diamonds is basically stable, but some stones can change color if they come into contact with a jeweler's torch.

The main advantage to buying irradiated diamonds is price. They're a fraction of the cost of fancy color diamonds. As a result more people can enjoy colored diamonds.

A big disadvantage is that even though they usually cost more than other colored gems, irradiated diamonds are hard to resell, so don't buy them as an investment. Potential buyers normally want natural-color diamonds.

Color treatment can sometimes be detected with magnification. Concentrations of color (color zoning) may be present along the facets or girdle or around the culet. Diamonds have characteristic color spectrums which also help gemologists determine the origin of their color. It's usually hard for a jeweler to prove that diamond color is natural. Therefore, when buying a fancy color diamond, get a report from a major gem laboratory stating that it's of natural color and origin, and purchase it from a knowledgeable, ethical seller.

High Pressure High Temperature (HPHT) Treatment

HPHT treatment was first used to change the color of diamonds in the 1970's. Laboratories were able to produce yellow and green colors by heating diamonds to temperatures above 1900°C under extreme pressure. It wasn't until 1999 that the trade learned it was possible to turn inexpensive brown diamonds colorless using the same treatment process. Colorless HPHT diamonds produced by the General Electric company are sold under the brand name "Bellataire."

These colorless diamonds are sold in upscale stores and advertised in classy fashion magazines. You may even find the term "natural" in the ads, so you wouldn't expect that they're treated. Sellers will tell you that HPHT diamonds are very rare and have been restored to their intrinsic natural color under the same conditions as diamonds formed in the earth.

Gem color is produced in nature through irradiation, too; but the trade doesn't view irradiated diamonds as natural. Any time man intervenes to change the color and/or clarity of a gemstone through any process other than cutting or cleaning, the stone is considered to be treated.

The advantage of HPHT-treated colorless diamonds:

1. **They allow their producers to reap big profits**. Bargain-priced diamonds in low demand are transformed into diamonds with expensive color grades.

Disadvantages of HPHT colorless diamonds:

1. **They have little resale potential,** except perhaps to uninformed consumers and to gemologists who want to study their characteristics. Untreated diamonds are the ones in demand; enhanced diamonds aren't.

2. **They offer no financial advantage to consumers.** As of the publication date of this book, HPHT diamonds aren't being sold at discounted prices. That will probably change as more and more companies get involved in treating diamonds by the HPHT process. Price could become an advantage in the future, even though it isn't one now.

Until that time, what's the point of buying an HPHT-treated diamond when you can get a natural one of the same color, clarity and cut quality for the same price or less?

3. **They may not be as resistant to abrasions and chipping as untreated diamonds.** In his book *Gemstone Enhancement* (pg 43.) Dr. Kurt Nassau writes, "High temperature heat treatments may cause some materials to become more brittle and show more wear." The *GIA Gem Reference Guide* states on page 262 in the section on zircon, "Toughness: heat-treated stones—poor to fair; untreated stones—fair to good."

We don't know yet what effect high temperature heat treatment has on the durability of diamonds. We do know, however, that untreated diamonds with a good clarity are able to withstand a lifetime of wear. It doesn't make sense to buy an HPHT diamond for an everyday ring when attractive untreated diamonds are readily available.

4. **Retailers that sell them at non-discounted prices may lose repeat business** when their customers discover they've overpaid and not been given full information on the diamonds.

Colored HPHT treated diamonds were introduced to the market in 2000. Yellowish-green colors are the most common but other colors such as blue, pink and red are also being produced. Consumers who are unable to find natural stones in these colors now have the option of purchasing their HPHT treated counterparts. The asking price will determine whether they're a good buy or not.

Detecting diamonds treated by the HPHT process requires specialized skills and equipment. Your best insurance for getting a natural-color diamond is to get a report from a gem lab that is experienced in identifying irradiated and HPHT-processed diamonds. If the report states that the diamond is enhanced or processed, this means the diamond is treated.

In Europe, some gem labs use the term "enhancement" on their reports to refer to routine treatments that are well accepted on colored gems. "Treatment" is reserved for unaccepted treatments. This policy has the effect of turning "treatment" into a negative term when in fact it's a neutral term by dictionary definition. A treatment can be good or bad; it depends on the type of treatment and how it's done. It makes more sense to simply state on lab reports the type of treatment a stone has undergone. The buyer can then determine if it's acceptable or not.

"Treatment" is the standard term used in gemological literature and at conferences for any process done to improve the appearance of a gemstone, except for cutting and cleaning. If we try to avoid or ban its use with the general public, it could give the impression that the trade doesn't believe in full disclosure of treatments. There are plenty of jewelers who will discuss treatments and quality characteristics in plain language. Deal with them when you buy gems.

For more information on diamonds treated with high pressures and temperatures, consult:

Australian Gemmologist, October-December 2000

Gems & Gemology, Fall 1999, Winter 1999, Spring 2000, Summer 2000, Fall 2000

The Journal of Gemmology, April 2000, October 2000, April 2001

"Changing the Color of Diamonds: The High Pressure High Temperature Process Explained, Techniques and Identification," a free booklet by Branko Deljanin and Gregory Sherman. Published by EGL (European Gemological Laboratory), New York, NY (212) 730-7380.

10

Synthetic Diamonds

This (synthetic) diamond costs one tenth the price of this (natural) diamond, and he says it's every bit as real.

This was the introduction to a Dateline NBC television interview with synthetic gem supplier Tom Chatham on April 4, 1995. Viewers across America were told that they might soon be able to buy synthetic (lab-grown) diamonds for a fraction of the cost of natural diamonds. Unlike cubic zirconia, which is a diamond imitation, synthetic diamond has essentially the same chemical composition and properties as its natural counterpart. The synthetic stone, however, is synthesized in a laboratory, not mined from the ground. To create diamond, carbon is dissolved in a molten metal solvent (flux) under extremely high pressures and temperatures and is allowed to crystallize for a few days.

Synthetic diamonds date back to the early 1950's when the General Electric Corporation (GE) started producing tiny diamonds that were used as industrial abrasives. In 1970, GE announced the creation of cuttable, gem-quality diamonds. Since then, others such as DeBeers, Sumitomo Electric Industries in Japan and a few Russian laboratories have also produced diamonds, which have been used industrially for precision cutting tools, miniature spacecraft windows, and heat sinks in electronic equipment. The diamonds are typically yellow to brownish yellow in color.

An article in the Spring 1997 issue of *Gems & Gemology* (pp. 42-59) showed some near colorless diamonds that had been grown for experimental purposes. The authors stated in the conclusion: "Because of technical challenges and the high cost of production, we question the likelihood that fashioned near-colorless synthetic diamonds over 25 points will enter the jewelry industry in commercial quantities. In our opinion the greatest possibility is the availability of near-colorless melee, because at these small sizes synthetic diamonds can be grown relatively fast and efficiently."

Limited quantities of loose synthetic diamonds have been sold and displayed at gem shows since the late 90's. They come in a variety of colors—yellow, blue, red, orangy yellow and greenish yellow, some of which are the result of treatment processes. Since synthetic diamonds are not produced in large quantities, you're not likely to find them for sale at your local jewelry store. That could change.

Lab-grown gemstones are not new. According to research scientist Kurt Nassau, by 1907, synthetic ruby was being produced at a total rate of some five million carats per year (*Gems Made by Man,* p. 27). Many other gems such as sapphire, emerald, amethyst, alexandrite and opal are also produced synthetically and sold in jewelry.

Fig. 10.1 Faceted and rough synthetic diamonds in different colors. *Copyright 1995 GIA & Tino Hammid.*

To the average consumer, the term "synthetic" means "fake." As a result, marketers of synthetic gems prefer to describe them as **created** or **lab-grown**. Created diamonds and synthetic diamonds are the same thing.

Cultured is sometimes used as a synonym for "lab-grown." The two terms, however, are not equivalent. Culturing pearls is a more natural process than growing gems.

Synthetic Versus Natural

Both natural and synthetic diamonds are essentially crystallized carbon, and they have the same hardness, luster and refractive qualities. However, there will be some important commercial differences, namely:

Price: Although lab-grown diamonds currently may cost almost as much as natural diamonds, their price is supposed to drop as production increases and technology improves. They might eventually sell for about one-tenth the cost of a natural diamond of the same clarity, color and cut.

Initially, synthetic ruby cost about as much as its natural counterpart. Today you can buy the same type of lab-grown ruby for less than a couple of dollars a carat. When well-cut, it can be quite attractive.

Growing Time: A 2-carat synthetic diamond takes less than a week to grow. Geologists tell us that diamonds were formed at least millions of years ago.

Emotional Value: Diamonds have traditionally had an aura of mystery due to their long, intriguing history and the remote places in which they are mined. Consumers interested in the romantic aspects of diamonds will generally attach a greater emotional value to a natural diamond than one created quickly in a laboratory. To them, there may be no substitute for the "real thing."

Potential for Price Appreciation: Despite market fluctuations, the overall value of natural diamonds has increased over the years. As a result, they've been accepted as a medium of exchange and a collateral for loans. Created gems have not enjoyed this prestige. Instead, their price has generally gone down as production and competition have increased. It's likely that the price of lab-grown diamond will follow suit. Rather than being viewed as a portable treasure, synthetic diamonds will be considered an affordable alternative to the natural stone.

Detecting Synthetic Diamonds

By law, synthetic gems must be disclosed to buyers. Unfortunately, there are unscrupulous sellers who try to pass off synthetics as being natural, so it's important to find ways to recognize them. Currently, the most reliable techniques for identifying lab-grown diamonds normally require specialized equipment and skill. De Beers, gem labs and diamond dealers hope to develop an affordable, practical instrument of detection.

Listed briefly below are some of the clues used to spot lab-grown diamonds. Keep in mind that the characteristics of synthetics vary depending on where and how they're grown.

Metallic inclusions. To the naked eye, these may look like tiny dark spots within the stone. They result if bits of the molten mixture used to grow the diamonds get trapped in the crystals. Magnification and experience are needed to distinguish these metallic inclusions from the dark spots sometimes seen in natural diamonds.

Magnetism. Due to the presence of metallic inclusions, synthetic diamonds may be attracted to or repelled by special magnets (fig. 10.2). Natural diamonds are not magnetic.

Unique raised or indented patterns on the surface of the stone (technically called **surface graining**). For example,

Fig. 10.2 A synthetic diamond attracted to a magnet. *Photo by Alan Hodgkinson.*

faint lines in the shape of an octagon might be visible on the top facet when light is reflected off the surface of the stone. Magnification is necessary. This surface graining can be hard to locate and it's not always seen in faceted synthetic diamonds; but when present, it serves as a good visual clue to the experienced observer.

Distinctive patterns of color when placed under an ultraviolet lamp and/or when immersed in a liquid such as methylene iodide. Magnification is normally required. Figure 10.3 illustrates some typical patterns seen in Russian synthetic diamonds. The trade term for uneven coloration is **color zoning**. Color zoning also occurs in natural diamonds but not in these types of patterns.

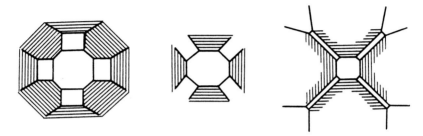

Fig. 10.3 Three patterns of color zoning seen in some Russian synthetic diamonds. This diagram is from an article in the Winter 1993 issue of *Gems & Gemology* entitled *"The Gemological Properties of Russian Gem-Quality Synthetic Yellow Diamonds." Courtesy Gemological Institute of America.*

Distinctive ultraviolet fluorescence, often stronger to short-wave than to long-wave ultraviolet (UV) light. In addition, the fluorescence is unevenly distributed.

A pronounced glow (phosphorescence) in colorless synthetic diamonds, when the UV lamp is turned off.

In addition, synthetic diamond can be identified by more advanced equipment such as X-ray fluorescence, chemical analysis or infrared spectroscopy, which are found in gem-testing labs.

If you don't have experience examining diamonds under magnification, the preceding clues are not very helpful. They do give you an idea, though, of how jewelers will spot synthetics. At the present, it's very unlikely you'll come across a colorless lab-grown diamond. However, be suspicious of intensely colored diamonds. Either they may be synthetic and/or their color may be the result of irradiation and heat treatment. Most of the synthetic diamonds examined by labs so far have been deep yellow, although some have been near colorless, red, blue or yellow-green.

When lab-grown diamonds are sold commercially, you'll be able to protect yourself by getting reports from labs with equipment that detects synthetics. The most economical form of protection, though, will be to deal with trustworthy jewelers who place an importance on continuing education. Honest jewelers can unwittingly misidentify stones if they don't keep up with new developments in the gem industry. Make sure your diamond purchases turn out to be positive experiences by doing business with knowledgeable professionals.

11

Gold & Platinum

Gold and platinum have a lot in common. In their pure form they resist tarnishing and they're hypoallergenic. They're both very malleable and ductile so they can be easily hammered, rolled or drawn into wire without breaking. Consequently, gold and platinum are excellent jewelry metals. They're both rare; yet they're abundant enough so everyone can own some. Platinum, however, is rarer than gold.

Both metals are important to industry and the medical field. Construction companies use glass tinted with gold for modern skyscrapers to keep them cool in summer, by reflecting the sun. Platinum is used for catalytic converters, surgical instruments, furnace thermometers and petroleum refining. Dentists couldn't get along without gold and platinum.

Compared to other metals, gold and platinum are heavy and dense. The density (or specific gravity) of platinum is 21.4 and of gold, 19.3. (This means, for example, that a given quantity of gold weighs 19.3 times as much as an equal quantity of water at 4°C.) Copper and silver, by contrast, have densities of 8.9 and 10.6 respectively. When used in jewelry, gold is usually alloyed with copper and silver, thus bringing the specific gravities of 18K and 14K gold to about 15.5 and 13.5. In jewelry form, both metals have a good solid, heavy feel, but platinum surpasses all jewelry metals in terms of density and weight.

Overall, gold and platinum have more similarities than differences. Before discussing how they differ, let's learn some basic terminology.

Gold & Platinum Terminology

Alloy
A mixture of two or more metals made by melting them together. Gold, for example, is alloyed (combined) with metals such as silver, copper, zinc and nickel to reduce its cost and change characteristics such as its color and hardness. **Platinum alloys** are usually made by combining platinum with ruthenium, iridium, palladium, cobalt or copper.

Avoirdupois weight
The weight system used in the U.S. for food and almost everything else except precious metals and gems. One avoirdupois pound equals 16 ounces.

Fine gold
Gold containing no other elements or metals. It's also called pure gold or 24K (24 karat) gold and has a fineness of 999.

Fineness
The amount of gold or platinum in relation to 1000 parts. For example, gold with a fineness of 750 has 750 parts (75%) gold and 250 parts of other metals. An alloy with 95% platinum and 5% ruthenium has a fineness of 950.

Gram	The most widespread unit of weight for gold and platinum jewelry. See Table 11.1 for equivalent weights.
Karat (Carat)	A measure of gold purity. One karat is 1/24 pure, so 24 karats is pure gold. Do not confuse "karat," the unit of gold purity, with "carat," the unit of weight for gemstones. Outside the USA, "karat" is often spelled "carat," particularly in countries which are members of the British Commonwealth.
Pennyweight	Unit of weight equaling 1/20 of a troy ounce. In the Middle Ages it was the weight of a silver penny in Britain. Now pennyweight is used mainly in the American jewelry trade.
Platinum group metals (PGM)	Platinum and the five other metals which are chemically and physically similar and which are often deposited with it: palladium, iridium, osmium, rhodium and ruthenium.
Plumb Gold (KP)	Gold that has the same purity as the mark stamped on it. 14KP does *not* mean *plated* karat gold. "KP" means the gold purity isn't lower than three parts per thousand of the fineness marked on the item. In other words it means "accurate gold."
Precious metals	Gold, silver and the platinum group metals.
Pt	The chemical symbol for platinum. "Pt" and "Plat" are used as abbreviated marks for platinum when identifying the metal and fineness of platinum. For example, when 900 Pt or 900 Plat is stamped on a jewelry piece, it means that it contains at least 900 parts per thousand of pure platinum.
Pure gold	Same as fine gold
Quality mark	A set of numbers, letters, or symbols stamped on metal to indicate its type and content. For example 18K means 75% gold, 900 Plat means 90% platinum. In the U.S., jewelry which does not cross state lines has not been required to have a quality mark. Fineness and karat marks are quality marks.
Solid gold	Gold that is not hollow. Legally in the U.S., "solid gold" can only be used to refer to 24K gold. However, the term solid gold more commonly refers to karat gold which is not hollow or layered.
Trademark	A mark that indicates the manufacturer, importer or seller of an item. In the USA, trademarks must be registered with the Patent and Trademark Office, and trademarked items must have a quality mark.
Troy Ounce (oz t)	A unit of weight used in England and the U.S. for gold and silver.
Troy weight	The system of weights used in the U.S. and England for gold and silver in which 1 pound equals 12 ounces and 1 ounce equals 20 pennyweights. It should not be confused with avoirdupois weight. The terms for weight are clearer in Table 11.1.

Fig. 11.1 Platinum jewelry with 24 karat gold inlay. All the pieces were designed and hand crafted by Zsombor Antal. *Photo by Zsombor Antal.*

Fig. 11.2 Platinum rings from Stuller. *Photo from Platinum Guild International USA.*

Table 11.1 Weight Conversions	
1 pennyweight (dwt)	= 1.555 g = 0.05 oz t = 0.055 oz av = 7.776 cts
1 troy ounce (oz t)	= 31.103 g = 1.097 oz av = 20 dwt = 155.51 cts
1 ounce avoirdupois (oz av)	= 28.3495 g = 0.911 oz t = 18.229 dwt = 141.75 cts
1 carat (ct)	= 0.2 g = 0.006 oz t = 0.007 oz av = 0.1286 dwt
1 gram (g)	= 5 cts = 0.032 oz t = 0.035 oz av = 0.643 dwt

Karat Value (Gold Fineness)

The purity of gold is described by its **fineness**, parts per 1000, or by the **karat**, a 1/24 part of pure gold by weight. (The spelling "carat" is used in the British Commonwealth). Pure gold is **alloyed** (combined) with other metals to make it more durable and affordable or to change its color. The table below lists karat qualities of gold jewelry.

Table 11.2 Gold Content and Notation			
USA Karat Stamping	Parts Gold	Gold %	Europe Fineness Stamping
24K	24/24	99.9%	999
22K	22/24	91.7%	916 or 917
18K	18/24	75.0%	750
14K	14/24	58.3%	583 or 585
12K	12/24	50.0%	500
10K	10/24	41.7%	416 or 417
9K	9/24	37.5%	375

In France and Italy, gold must be at least 18K to be called gold. In the U.S. and Japan, the legal standard is 10K; in Spain, Britain and Japan—9K; and in Germany—8K. The two most common qualities of gold are 14K and 18K with 18K being the international standard for higher quality jewelry. In India and Southeast Asia, 22K gold is popular because people there regard it as a monetary investment and like its deep yellow color. It's also becoming popular in Europe and North America along with 24K and 990 gold, which is normally hardened with titanium.

Fig. 11.3 This impressive diamond and black jade suite was made with mesh gold, which is a trademark style of Scott Keating. *Photo from Scott Keating Designs.*

Which is Better—14K or 18K Gold?

You may wonder whether 14K or 18K gold is better. 18K rings have 3/4 gold and 1/4 other material whereas 14K is just a little more than half gold. Consequently, rings with 18K gold are more valuable. They're also less likely to cause a reaction in people who are allergic to metals alloyed with gold, and they usually have a deeper yellow color than 14K gold. However, some 18K gold alloys may not be as hard and strong as 14K gold.

Rings of 14K gold are less expensive and often wear better. In North America, you'll probably have a better selection of 14K jewelry because a greater variety of it is manufactured. However, 14K might have a tendency to discolor or tarnish due to the lower percentage of gold and high percentage of copper. Occasionally, the metals alloyed with 14K gold cause an allergic reaction in some people.

Much of the better jewelry is made in 18K gold or in platinum. More and more jewelry of 22K, 24K or 990 gold is becoming available. Now that the price of gold is relatively low, high-purity gold can be a good buy. It's hypoallergenic and resists tarnish, and some of the new alloys are relatively durable. If you have a ring custom made, you can choose the gold percentage.

Have a look at some 14K, 18K and higher-karat gold rings. Usually there's some difference in color. Consider your color preferences along with the above points when choosing the karat quality. More often than not, the determining factor will be whether or not you can find a ring you like in your price range.

Platinum Content & Notation

Throughout the world, the purity of platinum is described only in terms of fineness. The markings and alloys used, however, may vary slightly. In 1997, the U.S. Federal Trade Commission established the following guidelines for platinum markings:

♦ 950 parts or more per thousand of pure platinum can be marked "platinum" without the use of any qualifying statements

♦ 850 to 950 parts per thousand can be marked in accordance with international standards of "950 Plat" or "950 Pt," "900 Plat" or "900 Pt," "850 Plat" or "850 Pt." Two- or four-letter abbreviations for platinum are permitted.

♦ 500 parts per thousand of pure platinum and at least 950 parts per thousand platinum group metals (iridium, osmium, palladium, rhodium and ruthenium) can be marked with the parts per thousand of pure platinum followed by the parts per thousand of each platinum group metal (example "600Plat 350Irid" or "600Pt 350Ir)

♦ less than 500 parts per thousand pure platinum cannot be marked with the word platinum or any abbreviation thereof.

In Canada, "**PLATINE**" (the French word for platinum) may also be used as a mark to indicate that an article contains at least 95% platinum.

Fig. 11.4 Platinum and 18K yellow gold jewelry from Michael Bondanza. *Photo by JQ Magazine, courtesy of the Platinum Guild International USA.*

In most European countries, platinum must have a purity of 95%. The typical markings are **Pt 950** or **950 Pt**. Occasionally, platinum chain products are made with 85% platinum and are marked Pt 850.

Sometime you'll see markings such as Pt 950 / 750. This means that part of the piece is 95% platinum and part is 18K gold. Gold and platinum combinations and accents are popular on jewelry now. See figures 11.1 and 11.8. Platinum is normally combined with gold that ranges from 18K to 24K. Gold that's 14K is usually combined with 14K white gold when a two-color look is desired. When buying combination-metal rings, ask if there will be a sizing problem. Sizing is normally not recommended if the entire shank has a two-color pattern.

Which is Better—A White Gold, Yellow Gold or Platinum Setting?

When choosing the setting for an expensive gemstone, the question often arises as to what metal would hold the stone most securely. The answer depends on the alloy used.

Alloyed platinum is denser and usually stronger (less likely to break or crack) than most gold alloys; but because of its high purity, platinum is a little softer than most gold alloys without palladium. Both gold and platinum are relatively soft in their pure form, with gold being the softest of the two. However, they become harder as certain alloying metals are added. A 95% gold alloy would typically be softer than one which is 95% platinum. But their hardness and strength would vary depending on the metals with which they're alloyed.

Platinum settings resist breakage, chipping and cracking better than those of gold. They can be more delicate, yet secure, provided they're hand fabricated or die stamped and not cast. Most platinum alloys retain their finish better and do not wear down the way gold does. This is due to the greater density and strength of platinum. In fact, some European insurance companies won't insure diamonds over one carat if they're not set in platinum because they know platinum settings are more secure.

Even though platinum rings should normally have platinum settings, it's appropriate for gold jewelry to have either gold or platinum settings. White gold settings are often used on yellow gold rings to provide a harder and more secure setting than yellow gold. The white gold can also enhance colorless diamonds. The same effect can be achieved by plating yellow-gold prongs with rhodium, a hard, white, highly reflective metal of the platinum family. The plating will wear off, though, and will need to be redone later. Another drawback of rhodium plating is that it makes jewelry more difficult to repair because the rhodium layer will burn in the heat of the soldering torch, flaking off the jewelry piece and making it impossible for the solder to flow. Solder only flows on a clean surface. Therefore before any heating takes place, the rhodium has to be removed from the surface. This is costly and time consuming. To avoid repair and replating problems, it's best to select platinum for white metal settings. It's both durable and white throughout.

Nickel white gold alloys are strongly discouraged in Europe. In the late 1980's, the European Union of the Common Market started the No-Nickel Policy in jewelry because it's estimated that perhaps 30% of all people are allergic to nickel to some extent. For example, you may get itchy or infected ears after wearing pierced earrings with nickel white gold or nickel-silver posts. Skin irritations from nickel zippers and jean buttons have been common too. Nickel

Fig. 11.5 A collection of three "Boundary Waters" series rings designed by artist and designer Eve J. Alfillé. These rings are created in 18 karat gold with princess-cut, triangular, and round diamonds. *Photo by Charles Hodges.*

Fig. 11.6 Three rings of 18K gold with mokume-gane designs of palladium and 18K yellow gold. Mokume-gane is an ancient Japanese technique of making wood grain patters with different types of metal. Wade Miley, who created these rings, says mokume-gane embodies the symbolism of marriage. There are two individual elements, distinct colors of metal, that are perfectly intertwined. The individual elements follow a path together but never lose their unique identity. *Photo by Azad.*

was originally chosen as a preferred alloying element for white gold because it was inexpensive and easy to work with. However, because of new health regulations, European refiners are avoiding the use of nickel and are creating different alloys with working qualities similar to nickel white gold. Companies who want to export white gold products to Europe are also modifying their white gold alloys.

Yellow gold is an appropriate setting for yellowish diamonds because it can mask their yellowish tints. If a diamond is so yellow that it can be classified as a fancy color, a platinum setting would be better. The white metal would emphasize the yellow of the diamond.

Platinum versus White Gold Jewelry

Platinum was the preferred white precious metal for American bridal jewelry between 1900 and 1940. When World War II began, the U.S. government declared platinum a strategic metal and banned its use in non-military applications such as jewelry. As a result, white gold was substituted as a precious white metal in jewelry. It's important to note that white gold and platinum are not at all the same. Platinum is naturally white whereas white gold is created from pure gold by adding other metals such as palladium or nickel, copper, zinc and silver. Since the white gold alloy is not completely white, it needs to be plated with a metal called rhodium to achieve the high white luster of platinum. This rhodium plating will eventually wear off, requiring additional plating to maintain the white effect of platinum.

Today, platinum is experiencing a tremendous resurgence of popularity as consumers rediscover its beauty and benefits. Its neutral color enhances diamonds and other gemstones. Thanks to its strength and density, platinum holds diamonds securely and has a high resistance to wear. This is why platinum prong settings are frequently used on gold rings and why estate jewelry made of platinum often looks relatively new after many years of wear. White gold is not as durable as platinum. Sometimes white gold prong settings must be retipped to maintain security for the gemstone placed in the setting.

The major advantage of white gold is price. In 2001, for example, an 18K nickel white gold wedding band cost about one-third to one-fourth the price of a platinum band the same size. This is not just because platinum sells for more than gold. Platinum bands normally have a higher purity (usually 90–95%) than gold bands, which are typically 55.3% to 75% gold. In addition, platinum is more compact and dense than white gold. Consequently a platinum band would weigh more than a white gold band. And the more the metal weighs, the more it costs.

The price of platinum wasn't always as high as it is now. In January 1996, platinum was $418 an ounce and gold $395 an ounce. Five years later, in May 2001, platinum was selling for $617 an ounce and gold $266. The high platinum prices are making white gold more attractive to people on limited budgets. Palladium, a platinum group metal which is sometimes alloyed with platinum and gold, has typically cost less than platinum. However at certain times in 2001 it sold for over $1000 an ounce, thereby discouraging its use in white gold.

Another advantage of gold is its lower weight. White gold earrings, for example, are lighter and therefore more comfortable than platinum earrings of the same style and size. The advantages and disadvantages of white gold and platinum are summarized in Table 11.3:

Fig. 11.7 Platinum and platinum/18K gold rings copyrighted by Studio E. *Photo from PGI USA.*

Fig. 11.8 Platinum rings by Michael Francis with splash 24K gold and 24K gold inlay. *Photo from PGI USA.*

Table 11.3

White Gold	Platinum (Pt)
Costs a great deal less than platinum. Nickel white gold costs less than palladium white gold.	In 2001, pure platinum cost more than double the price of pure gold. Pt 950 cost more than three times as much as 14K nickel white gold.
Nickel white gold may be a bit yellowish so needs to be plated with rhodium to resemble platinum. Palladium white gold may be slightly yellowish or a darker gray than platinum. It's often rhodium plated but not always. The rhodium plating complicates repair work, and it can wear off.	Platinum does not require rhodium plating, but it's sometimes plated to conceal solder joints.
Weighs less than platinum. The density of 24K (pure) gold = 19.32 14K nickel white gold ranges from ≈ 13 to 14 14K palladium white gold ≈ 13.5 to 14.5 18K nickel white gold ≈ 14.5 to 15.5 18K palladium white gold ≈ 15.5 to 16.5	Is heavier than white gold. The density of 99.9 Pt = 21.4 95% Pt 5% iridium = 21.4 95% Pt 5% cobalt = 20.8 90% Pt 10% iridium = 21.5 90% Pt 10% palladium = 19.8
Pure gold is softer than pure platinum. Nickel white gold is harder and more scratch resistant than platinum alloys; palladium white gold has a similar hardness to platinum alloys.	Pure platinum is harder than pure gold. 95 Pt is softer and less scratch-resistant than nickel white gold but is similar in hardness to palladium white gold.
Pure gold is hypoallergenic; some people have an allergic reaction to nickel white gold.	Pure platinum and alloys of platinum are hypoallergenic.
Nickel white gold is susceptible to stress cracking and stress corrosion from chlorine and from the heat of soldering. Don't wear white gold in hot-tubs and swimming pools because the chlorine can attack the metal. Palladium white gold is not as strongly affected by chlorine as nickel white gold.	Platinum and platinum alloys are not affected by chlorine and they don't exhibit the cracking problems and brittleness of nickel white gold. Therefore platinum settings are more secure.
Pure gold, high-karat gold and rhodium plated white gold don't tarnish. When rhodium plating wears away, the yellowish tint of the unplated white gold can show through. Palladium white gold resists tarnish better than nickel white gold.	Platinum and platinum alloys without copper do not tarnish or discolor. Most platinum in Europe and North America is alloyed with iridium, ruthenium or cobalt. In Japan, Europe and Hong Kong, palladium is also used in platinum alloys.
White gold is more resistant to wear and abrasions than yellow gold but not as resistant as platinum because of the lower density of gold.	Platinum jewelry lasts and resists abrasion better than gold jewelry because the platinum molecules are more compact and dense.

This table is based on information in *Jewellry Technology* by Diego Pinton, *The Mountings Book* from Stuller, "Platinum Alloys and Their Application in Jewelry Making" by PGI USA, written by Jurgen Maerz, *Professional Goldsmithing* by Alan Revere, and *Working in Precious Metals* by Ernest Smith.

For further information on gold, platinum, alloys, fineness and craftsmanship, consult the *Gold & Platinum Jewelry Buying Guide: How to Judge, Buy, Test & Care for It* by Renée Newman.

12

Choosing an Appropriate Setting Style

What setting style is best for your diamond(s) and why? To answer this question, you'll need to know what styles there are to choose from and what advantages each has to offer. This chapter describes basic styles and lists their positive and negative points.

PRONG (CLAW) SETTING: This is the most common type of setting, especially for ladies' solitaire diamond rings (fig 12.1). It involves fitting the diamond in a metal head or basket and securing it with a minimum of three prongs or metal claws. The shape of the prongs can vary. They may be rounded, elongated or pointed. There are many decorative variations of this setting style.

Advantages of prong setting:

♦ It allows more of the stone to be in view than most other styles.

♦ It's quicker and, therefore, less expensive to set than most other styles.

♦ Can hold large diamonds securely. Small diamonds (less than 0.10 ct) may fall out with hard wear because often, they're not set with the same care as a larger, more prominently displayed stone.

Fig. 12.1 Prong (claw) settings. *Rings from Gabrielle Diamonds; photo from Suberi Bros.*

Settings with six prongs are more secure than those with four. If a prong is damaged on a 4-prong setting, it's easy to lose the stone. But, if one is damaged on a 6-prong setting, the stone will probably stay in until the setting can be repaired.

♦ Allows the diamonds to be more easily cleaned than the other styles—provided the prongs are not encased with a lot of metal or wire.

♦ Can be used to set any type of gemstone, no matter how fragile it is. Prong setting is particularly popular for transparent faceted gemstones.

Disadvantages of prong setting:

♦ May not provide as smooth of a ring surface as some of the other styles. Sometimes, the prongs have a tendency to get caught in clothing and hair, especially if the setting is high. The

Fig. 12.2 High prong-setting

Fig. 12.3 The lower settings in these rings are more practical. *Rings from Mark Schneider, photo by Daniel Rossen.*

owner of the engagement ring in figure 12.2 wishes it had a lower setting. She was unable to wear the ring while her children were young because it would scratch and hurt them. In addition, the setting has snagged her nylons and sweaters. Prong settings don't have to be high. Figure 12.3 shows two prong-set rings that are lower and more practical. The center ring has a partial bezel setting.

◆ Doesn't protect diamonds as well as other styles since it leaves most of the girdle area exposed. V tips can help protect the points of marquise, heart and pear shape stones (fig 12.4).

Fig. 12.4 A V-tip protects the point of this prong-set diamond. *Ring & photo from Gary Dulac.*

Fig. 12.5 Channel-set diamonds. *Ring & photo from Varna.*

CHANNEL SETTING: This style is often used for wedding bands (fig. 12.5), but it may also be used to accent center stones (fig. 12.3). The diamonds are suspended in a channel of vertical walls with no metal separating the stones.

Fig. 12.6 Bezel setting protects the edge of stones well and normally needs no repair. *Rings from Michael Francis; photo from Platinum Guild International USA.*

Fig. 12.7 Partial bezels. *Rings from Wade Miley Designer Jewelry; photo by Azad.*

Advantages of channel setting:

♦ Protects the girdle area of the diamonds.

♦ Provides a smooth ring surface.

♦ Is appropriate for enhancing ring shanks and for creating linear designs with a tailored look.

Disadvantages of channel setting:

♦ Usually more time consuming and costly than prong setting, when properly done. Some channel setting is done cheaply and quickly by just cutting a long groove in thin metal and sliding diamonds in, but the stones may not be secure. In good channel setting, the stones are placed individually in seats in a sturdy channel with sufficient metal along both sides of the channel to support them well.

♦ Risky, in terms of damage to stones, so should not be used for fragile gems.

BEZEL (TUBE) SETTING: A bezel is a band of metal that surrounds the diamond and holds it in place. In the past, bezel settings were used mostly for cabochons (unfaceted, dome-shaped stones) such as jade and star sapphire. They have become popular now as attractive settings for diamonds. The bezel may either fully or partially encircle the stone (figs. 12.6 & 12.7).

Advantages of bezel setting.

♦ Provides good protection for the girdle and pavilion areas of diamonds.

♦ Can be used to set almost all gemstones without causing damage to them.

♦ When done properly, holds diamonds well and doesn't require repairing later on. Jeweler Michael Francis of Seattle likes to bezel set stones in bridal rings (fig. 12.6) because he believes they should be functional and last forever. If he does do a prong style, he makes sure the prongs are thick enough to last.

Eric Walls, a jewelry designer from Boulder, Colorado, likes bezel settings too. He says they never wear out or need repair or maintenance. He often does partial bezel settings to reveal more of the stones and to allow more light into them.

♦ Accentuates the circumference of the stone, making it appear larger than in prong setting.

♦ The bezel setting provides a smooth ring surface.

Disadvantages of bezel setting:

♦ Usually more time consuming and expensive than prong and bead setting.

BEAD or PAVE SETTING: In this type of setting, diamonds are fit into tapered holes and set almost level with the surface of the ring. Then some of the surrounding metal is raised to form beads which hold the diamonds in place. This style is frequently used for women's rings (fig. 12.8) Sometimes the metal around the bead-set stones is raised or engraved to form decorative patterns.

When there are three or more rows of diamonds set in this way without partitions between the stones, it is called *pavé*, which, in French, means *paved* like a cobblestone road. The jewelry trade often refers to any type of bead setting as pavé. In order to give the impression of a continuous diamond surface, it is customary to use white gold or platinum to support pavé-set diamonds even if the rest of the mounting is yellow gold. Rhodium plating is added to further heighten this effect. If diamonds are yellowish, they tend to look better set in yellow gold without rhodium plating.

Fig. 12.8 Three rows of pavé-set diamonds and a semi-circular row of bead-set diamonds accent the sides of this ring. The center diamond is set in a partial flush setting. *Photo and ring from the James Vilona Platinum Collection.*

Advantages of bead or pavé setting:

♦ Usually protects diamonds better than prong setting.

♦ Allows uninterrupted designs of varying width. When pavé designs are spread over the surface of a mounting, they can make the diamonds appear larger and more numerous than they actually are.

Disadvantages of bead or pavé setting:

♦ Is a risky setting method in terms of possible stone damage. Good diamonds, rubies, and sapphires can withstand the pressure of being pavé set, but fragile stones such as emeralds, opals, tourmalines and diamonds with large cracks risk damage.

♦ Doesn't provide as smooth of a ring surface as bezel, channel and flush setting.

♦ May not be as secure as other settings.

FLUSH SETTING. Flush setting is a popular style for people who use their hands a lot in their professions; it offers good protection for their diamonds. The stone is fit snugly into a tapered hole that is grooved to hold the girdle of the stone. Then the surrounding metal is pressed and hammered around the rim of the opening to secure the diamond (fig. 12.9). When a center stone is flush set in a moderate to high dome at the top of the ring, it's called a gypsy setting,

Advantages of flush setting:

♦ Protects the girdle area of diamonds.

♦ When done properly, holds diamonds well.

♦ Provides a smooth, tailored look.

Fig. 12.9 Flush-set fancy-color diamonds accent the prong-set center stone. The ring by Varna has a sandblasted finish and shiny engraving.

Disadvantages of flush setting:

♦ Is usually more time consuming and expensive than prong and bead setting.

♦ Is a very risky setting method, in terms of damage to stones, so it should not be used for fragile gems.

BAR SETTING: This is a form of channel setting, except the stones are set in channels across a ring, and the stones on each end of the channel are exposed at the edges of the mounting instead of being secured in metal. As a result, the bar-set stones can get loose or chipped with repeated banging. Channel setting is more secure because the channel is enclosed with metal at each end. Otherwise bar setting has the same advantages as channel setting.

Fig. 12.10 Side and top of a bar-set mounting. *Photo from Stuller.*

INVISIBLE SETTING: Invisible-set diamonds are placed tightly next to each other with the metal of the setting concealed underneath the diamonds, allowing them to form a continuous surface (fig.12.11). The initial development of invisible setting was credited to Jacques Albert-Algier, a French jeweler, and the style was popularized by Cartier and Van Cleef & Arpel. Square rubies and sapphires were the first stones to be invisibly set. In the mid 1980's, Israel Itzkowitz and Betz Ambar of Ambar Diamonds in Los Angeles perfected a method of invisible setting for square diamonds. They claim to be the first to set diamonds invisibly.

This setting style became so popular that Ambar Diamonds decided in the mid 1990's to find a way to set round stones with the same technique. After long and tedious research, they developed and patented a method of invisible setting for round stones. This new round setting style is sold under the trademarked name "Boundless" (fig. 12.12).

Fig. 12.11 Invisible-set Quadrillion® diamonds. *Photo from Ambar Diamonds.*

Fig. 12.12 Invisible-set (Boundless®) round diamonds. *Photo
and rings from Ambar Diamonds.*

Advantages of invisible setting:

◆ Emphasizes the diamonds more than other styles since the metal setting is concealed.

◆ Enhances brilliance because there's no metal on the top of the stone to impede the entry of light.

◆ Allows jewelry designers to create a smooth, uninterrupted diamond surface with square stones.

Disadvantages of invisible setting:

◆ It costs more than most other setting styles because it requires expensive machinery and highly skilled setters.

◆ If not properly set, small square stones may fall out with hard wear.

◆ Not many setters know how to do and repair invisible setting, particularly with round stones. **Make sure that the store who sells you invisibly-set jewelry will service it for you**.

An awareness of the benefits and drawbacks of the various setting styles can be helpful in choosing diamond jewelry. To see how, let's look at the following examples:

◆ Connor is a construction engineer. He wants a diamond wedding ring that he can wear as much as possible.

Connor might consider choosing a sturdy flush-set diamond ring. The low, flush setting could help protect his diamond from the unusual abuse it might get if he forgot to take it off during work or if he chose not to take it off. A gypsy- or bezel-set ring could also be suitable, but Connor should avoid high prongs and settings which leave the girdle edge of the diamond exposed to knocks.

Fig. 12.13 Left: invisible-set, rounded Quadril-lions®; center & right: bar-set Quadrillions® in an eternity ring with baguettes on the sides to give it a three dimensional look. *Photo and rings from Ambar Diamonds.*

Fig. 12.14 Floating Diamonds™ semi-mount and band by Peter Storm. It took Peter two years to develop the process of setting princess cuts point to point in a channel. Each diamond is supported by an under carriage so it can't shift and become loose. This trademarked setting style provides a distinctive look and requires fewer diamonds than traditional channel setting. *Photo from Peter Storm Designs.*

♦ Charlene is looking for a dinner ring with lots of flash. She doesn't have enough money for a large diamond.

Charlene might consider getting a pavé-diamond ring or one with a cluster of small prong-set diamonds. Either type of ring could display an impressive, sparkling mass of brilliance.

♦ Sandy is active in contact sports and is hard on jewelry. She wants a diamond ring that would be suitable for everyday wear and she doesn't want to have to take it off when she does household chores and other work.

Sandy might consider buying a ring with a center diamond that's bezel set and side stones that are flush set. The ring could be very smooth so it wouldn't scratch other players if she forgot to take it off during a game, and there wouldn't be as much risk of the diamonds falling out due to broken prongs or beads.

Fig. 12.15 Bezel & flush set diamonds in a ring by Richard Kimball. *Photo by Azad.*

It's not common practice for jewelry buyers to analyze what setting styles would be best and why, but it should be. Too often, jewelry that looks attractive when bought turns out to be impractical. With a bit of forethought, it's possible to select a style that is not only aesthetically pleasing but functional as well. However, no matter how suitable the style, if a stone is not properly set, there could be durability problems. To avoid them, deal with jewelers who place an importance on good craftsmanship.

13

Choosing a Diamond Ring

The Significance of the Diamond Ring

Think of a circle. It has no beginning or end. Think of a knot tied around your finger. It binds and reminds. And so it is with a ring. It reminds you of an eternal binding commitment to a lover, spouse, friend, school, church, club or country.

The commitment to marry a woman is usually expressed by placing a ring on her fourth finger. This custom may have originated with the Egyptians. They believed a special vein or nerve ran from that finger to the heart. Another explanation for the custom is that it may have been a suggestion to women that they should be submissive to their future husbands since the fourth finger is the weakest one and can't be used independently. A third explanation is that placing the ring on the fourth finger may have been a way to avoid damaging the ring since it is the best-protected finger.

Diamonds were probably first added to wedding and engagement rings in the 15th century. To the upper class Europeans of this period, diamonds represented fortitude, innocence, prosperity and faithfulness. They assumed that a diamond's power to withstand natural forces could be transferred to the owners and that they, in turn, would be able to withstand temptation and adversity. Religious and cultural beliefs outside of Europe also contributed to the mystique of the diamond. The Hindus felt that offering a diamond to Krishna was a guarantee of eternal life in the highest heaven. Buddhists used the diamond as a symbol of spiritual balance, peace of mind, clarity of thought and unlimited insight. In addition to its spiritual meanings, the diamond's remarkable hardness made it more resistant to wear than other gems, and its neutral color allowed it to be worn with any color of clothing and with any other gemstones.

Rather than a pin, necklace, earring or bracelet, a ring is used traditionally as a pledge of marriage. Aside from its symbol as an eternal commitment of love, a ring can be worn anytime anywhere without getting in the way, and you don't need a mirror to enjoy it.

Choosing a Ring Style

Many people choose a ring style only on the basis of how pretty it looks, and this is normal. However, you should also ask if the ring is:
♦ Flattering to your hand
♦ Suitable for your needs
♦ Comfortable
♦ Well-crafted
♦ Worth the price

In this chapter, the term **mounting** will often be used instead of "ring style." This is the term that the jewelry trade uses for rings before they are set with stones. Previous chapters have already suggested how to choose the shape of your diamond(s) and the setting style, so this chapter will be limited to the choice of mounting.

No matter how practical or valuable a ring is, there's no point in buying it if you don't like the style. Therefore you should naturally select a style that is attractive to you. When making your choice, ask yourself, too, if the mounting enhances the diamonds and if you will still love it in ten or twenty years.

Even though a ring may look attractive to you, it may not flatter your hand. **Do you have a small hand and short fingers?** A huge, broad ring can make your fingers look too short and your hand too small. To make your fingers look longer, you can choose a mounting with stones or lines arranged diagonally across or down the length of your finger. Otherwise you might wear simple rings with thin bands.

Do you have long thin fingers? Button and cluster styles and large broad rings can look good on your hands. A mounting with stones or lines flowing across your finger or that have height can make your hand look shorter.

Do you have long broad hands? A very small ring will tend to make them look bigger, so normally a larger ring is better. If you're a woman, simple or delicate designs should flatter your hand.

Do you have an average-size hand? You're fortunate. Almost any ring will look good on your hand. However, a ring that is too large can make your hand look smaller and defeat the advantage of having an ideal-size hand.

Besides flattering your hand, a ring should be **suitable for your needs**. If it's for everyday or business wear, a simple style will probably be best. If it's for dress, you might want something fancier. No matter where you intend to wear your ring, there are some practical things to consider for it to be suitable. When choosing a ring, ask yourself the following questions:

◆ Does the mounting have points and sharp edges which could cut you or damage your clothing or furniture? Often the points can be rounded off and the sharp edges filed or polished away, but sometimes there is nothing you can do to prevent a mounting from snagging your clothes. Even when the points are rounded off, a mounting can be impractical for daily wear. The owner of the ring in figure 13.1 wishes she had chosen a different style mounting. The portion that sticks out with the stone often gets caught on clothing, ledges and in doors. This jerks the ring up and makes the edge of the band dig into her finger.

◆ Is it easy to clean, especially if it's for everyday wear?

◆ If you live in a cold climate and need to wear gloves, can you slip them on without damaging your ring or ripping the gloves?

Fig. 13.1 An impractical design.

Fig. 13.2 Elegant yet practical. The entire surface of these rings is smooth so they don't catch on clothing or scratch people. Gloves can be worn over them without any problem. And the partial bezel settings should last a lifetime.

The ring on the right with the recessed setting offers the most protection for the diamond. *Rings & photo from Judith Conway.*

♦ Does the ring blend in with your other jewelry, if you plan to wear them together?

♦ Can the ring be sized easily? Does your weight or finger size change frequently? If so, pay attention to the sizing factor and avoid, for example, eternity rings that have stones all around the band. Instead choose a ring where at least one third of the band is unset metal.

   If you think your finger size could change by two or more sizes (this is unlikely), mention this to your jeweler and he will help you select an appropriate mounting. He'll probably suggest that you avoid rings with lots of baguette-shaped stones set up and down the sides of the mounting and tension settings (settings that secure the stone with pressure on opposite sides rather than just metal).

♦ Does your center diamond always flop to the side, or does the ring stay in an attractive position as your hand moves? This problem sometimes occurs when a large diamond is mounted on a ring. It can be corrected by choosing a wider band or a band that is square or oval in shape on the outside instead of round (fig. 4.5 on the next page). This problem can also occur if the ring is too big. Sizing balls inside the shank can help a ring stay in place on arthritic hands, which require oversize rings.

♦ Does your jewelry tend to show lots of scratches? People with active lifestyles often choose ring mountings with matte or brushed finishes because scratches and fingerprints are less noticeable.

   Matte (non-shiny) finishes can be added to any mounting. Figure 13.3 shows an example of a coarse brushed finish. If you prefer the brilliance of a shiny finish (fig. 13.5), you can have the scratches polished away if they become obvious. A little of the metal, however, can wear away with repeated polishing.

Fig. 13.3 A coarse brushed finish. *Rings and photo from Aaron Henry Design Goldsmith.*

Fig. 13.4 A-hand textured finish gives this jewelry a luxurious, sophisticated look and prevents fingerprints from showing. *Jewelry from Suna; photo from the Platinum Guild International USA.*

In figure 13.4, you'll see jewelry pieces with a hand-textured finish resembling a satin finish—a very finely brushed surface texture like satin.

♦ Does your ring look attractive from more than one angle? You don't just view your ring from the top. In fact, sometimes you look at it more often from the side when you're wearing it. Figures 13.6–13.9 on the next two pages show examples of rings designed to be viewed from a variety of angles.

Some of these practical considerations may not apply to you because of your special needs. One man who wanted a ring to serve as a weapon had it designed as a pyramid coming to a sharp point on top in order to enable him to rip the skin of an attacker as he punched him in the face. Liberace had a ring designed to look like a piano.

Fig. 13.5 Platinum ring with a shiny finish. *Photo from Platinum Guild International USA.*

Pretty Rings From All Viewing Angles

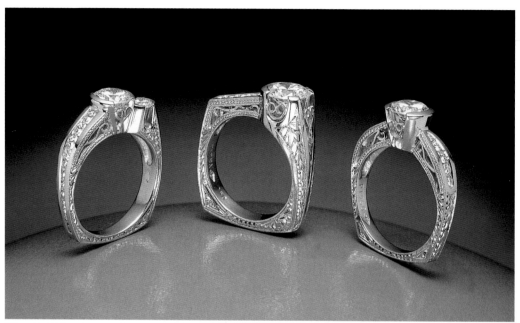

Fig. 13.6 Hand engraving, gold filigree (fine wirework) and asymmetrical designs add interest to all angles of these rings from Varna. The squarish bottoms are very comfortable and prevent the ring from flopping from side to side. *Photo from Varna.*

Fig. 13.7 Diamonds accent these platinum rings on the sides as well as on the top. These rings by Mark Schneider are attractive no matter how they're viewed. *Photo by Daniel Van Rossen.*

Pretty Rings From All Viewing Angles

Fig. 13.8 Diamonds and platinum mountings with flowing contours add beauty to all vantage points of these rings. *Photo and rings from the James Vilona Platinum Collection.*

Fig. 13.9 Some more original ring designs from Mark Schneider. These rings are in 18K gold. *Photo by Daniel Van Rossen.*

Fig. 13.10 Sturdy but feminine. The shanks and bezel settings of these rings have sufficient metal and the prongs are heavy gauge so they'll be able to withstand a lifetime of daily wear. Eric Wall, the creator of these rings, doesn't want customers to ever have a problem with his jewelry. Therefore he avoids very thin prongs and mountings. *Photo from Walls Design Ltd.*

◆ Does the mounting style protect the center stone? This is important for everyday rings. Ideally, if you accidentally hit your ring against walls or furniture, the contact will be with the metal of the ring and not the stones. If the stone(s) stick out past the contour of the ring, they're much more susceptible to damage than if they're recessed or within the outline of the ring.

◆ Is the band or the prongs so thin that they will wear down quickly if you wear the ring everyday? If you can bend the band easily with your fingers, it's probably too thin. Figure 13.10 shows examples of rings with prongs and partial bezels that have substantial metal.

Ring comfort may seem to be a matter of common sense. Yet, many people ignore this factor, particularly when they buy rings through mail-order or have them custom made. When choosing a ring ask yourself:

◆ Can you bend your fingers easily when wearing it? If not, the band may be too wide. Besides being uncomfortable, it could cause skin irritation due to collection of moisture and dirt under the band. If you like the wide-, broad-ring look, select a band that tapers down from a wide top to a narrow bottom so that your finger can bend freely.

◆ Is the ring too tight or too loose? This can be corrected by resizing the ring. If your band is more than 3/8" (10 mm.) wide, it will probably need to be a half size larger than what you normally wear in order to feel comfortable.

◆ Does the ring feel rough and scratchy? If the metal does, it can usually be smoothed down by polishing. Occasionally, diamonds are set too low and the pointed bottoms prick your finger. If this is the case, it would probably be easier to choose another ring than to correct the problem.

Besides being comfortable, engagement and wedding rings must be **well-crafted** in order to withstand everyday wear. It's not easy for a lay person to judge craftsmanship, but there are a few things that can provide clues about the overall workmanship. Check the ring for the following characteristics:

♦ Are the diamond(s) set securely? One of the most frequent problems with prong-setting is poorly seated stones. (The seat is a notch or groove in the prong which supports the stone). If a diamond is not flat against the seat, it won't be stable and well-supported. Occasionally, setters neglect to put in a seat; instead, they just bend over the prongs. A stone without a seat is not secure. The diagrams in figures 13.11 and 13.12 show examples of a well-set stone and a poorly seated stone.

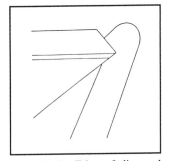

Fig. 13.11 Edge of diamond flat against the seat in the prong

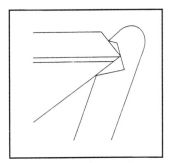

Fig. 13.12 Poorly seated stone

♦ If the ring has channel setting, are the channels straight? They shouldn't be wavy or uneven.

♦ Does the inside of the ring look smooth and clean? If not, this indicates a lack of attention to detail. Well-made pieces do not have rough finishes and jagged edges that can scratch you.

♦ Can you see the solder joints or excess solder? This is a sign of poor craftsmanship.

♦ Does the metal look pitted or cracked? This could be caused by improper casting and soldering, or by a poor quality alloy.

For a more thorough discussion of jewelry craftsmanship and proper setting, consult the *Gold & Platinum Jewelry Buying Guide* by Renée Newman. Besides providing more detailed information, it has lots of photos showing examples of both acceptable and inferior craftsmanship.

Once you've decided a ring is attractive, suitable, comfortable and well-crafted, you might wonder if it's **worth the price**. To determine this, you should know the factors that affect the cost of mountings. To understand these factors, you should become familiar with the following terms:

Cast **(Lost wax method)**	Refers to mountings made by thrusting molten metal into plaster-of-Paris type molds with a centrifugal force or vacuum. The mold is made by pouring the plaster-of-Paris type material over a wax model of the desired ring. The wax is then melted, leaving a ring mold.

Casting is a relatively fast process that allows many identical articles to be made from a single design, which is why most jewelry is made using this method. Cast mountings may be porous if they're not done with proper heat, timing and acceleration in clean machines free from contaminants. Mountings with tiny pinpoint holes (porosity) can have durability problems.

Die-struck (Stamped) Refers to mountings formed with metal parts mechanically punched out of compressed sheet metal with dies (forms or molds). Since this metal is hard, compact and non-porous, it has a good resistance to wear. Die-struck mountings generally have simple, standard designs and are produced in large quantities.

Hand-fabricated Refers to mountings made by sawing, filing and shaping metal parts and wire by hand and then soldering them together. A hand-fabricated mounting is usually *one of a kind* and typically takes a lot of time to make.

Custom-made Made for special order instead of mass-produced. Generally, *custom-made* refers to rings requiring handwork or individual casting and specially-made molds. It can also refer to rings formed by soldering prefabricated metal parts together to form a design chosen by a customer. If a customer has a ring modified by changing the stones, it is usually called a **remount**.

Factors Affecting the Cost of Mountings

♦ The higher the gold or platinum content, the greater the cost of the mounting. Therefore the weight of a mounting is an important cost factor.

♦ The value of the metal in the mounting increases as follows: 14 karat gold < 18 karat gold < 22 karat gold < platinum.

♦ Sometimes, white gold mountings cost slightly more than those of yellow gold because they're often made to order or manufactured in lower quantities, or the white gold alloy may be harder to cast without creating cracks in the metal. In addition, white gold requires rhodium plating.

♦ Mountings made of more than one component will cost more due to the labor involved in the assembly.

♦ Mountings engraved with the name of the designer or jeweler usually cost more than those without such an engraving.

♦ Mountings that require a lot of work to cast, shape or polish cost more than those that are quick and easy to finish.

♦ Custom-made mountings cost more than mass-produced mountings. If a jeweler has to make a mold and cast a ring individually, you can expect to pay at least double what it would have cost if it had been mass produced.

When you evaluate the cost of ring mountings, keep all the above factors in mind. Try to compare mountings of the same metal, weight and manufacturing process. Slight differences in

Fig. 13.13 A custom-designed diamond ring by Richard Kimball. *Photo by Azad.*

Fig. 13.14 Platinum & 24K gold inlay ring custom crafted and photographed by Zsombor Antal.

mountings do not normally affect the cost of a diamond ring much. In most cases, the major portion of the cost is in the diamonds. Slight, unnoticeable differences in diamond quality can have a large effect on the cost of a diamond ring.

Tips on Buying Custom-Made Rings

If you're unable to find a ready-made diamond ring that's attractive, comfortable and suitable for your needs, you might try having one custom made. Not only will your ring be unique, it will probably mean more to you if you participate in creating it. Having a ring made to order should be a positive experience, and you can help prevent it from turning into a disappointing one by taking the following precautions:

♦ Try on rings that resemble the one you want to have made. What looks good in a picture may not look or feel good on your hand.

♦ If possible, have good drawings, photos or models of the ring you want made. Never assume that the jeweler understands your verbal description of what you want.

♦ Don't assume a ring will look exactly like it does in a photo. It should, however, have a close resemblance. The best way to get exactly what you want is to have a model or a sample ring.

♦ Be as specific as possible about ring features that you consider important. For example, state in advance if you want the prongs holding your diamonds to be rounded off or hammered in a square or triangular form. Otherwise, the jeweler will assume that the prong style doesn't matter to you so long as the prongs are secure and uniform and don't cover too much of the diamonds.

You should also tell the jeweler beforehand if you want the inside of your ring to have a special look. In one instance, a lady wanted thin bars under every stone of a diamond eternity band instead of under every other stone. Unless jewelers are told otherwise, they will probably assume that as long as the inside of a ring is smooth and well polished, its appearance won't matter much to a customer since the inside doesn't show when the ring is worn.

♦ If you have a ring that fits well and has about the same band width as the custom ring you are ordering, show it to the salesperson or jeweler so they can choose the best ring size for you. The sample metal rings they have you try on can sometimes suggest the wrong size.

Fig. 13.15 A custom-made spinel ring accented by sapphires and diamonds. It was hand fabricated by Gary Dulac. *Photo by John Parrish.*

Fig. 13.16 Another custom-fabricated ring by Gary Dulac. It features a 2.60 carat tsavorite and is made of platinum and 18K gold. *Photo by John Parrish.*

♦ Always tell a jeweler you need the ring earlier than you actually do, especially if it's a complicated job. Work out an acceptable delivery date and have it put in writing. But still be prepared for delays. It's best not to rush custom-made jewelry.

♦ If possible, avoid having jewelry custom made in December in countries that celebrate Christmas. Since jewelers are rushed and overworked at that time of year, they might not do their best work then.

♦ Get a written estimate of the cost of the ring. If more diamonds are needed than estimated, the jeweler is not expected to give them to you free of charge. He should, however, get your permission before doing anything that would increase the estimated cost of the ring.

♦ Know in advance who will be responsible if your diamonds are lost or damaged during setting or recutting. If you give a jeweler your diamonds, he's not always liable if something unfortunate happens to them. Reliable jewelers, however, will either feel morally obligated to replace damaged or lost diamonds or else will clearly warn you that your diamonds are at risk.

♦ If the ring is being cast, check and try on the wax model before casting. Make sure you're happy with the height, width, and comfort of the ring. It's easier to make changes in a wax than in a cast piece.

♦ Know the refund policy of the jeweler. It's normal for jewelers to retain at least a portion of your deposit if you decide not to buy the ring you ordered, particularly if it's a style that would be difficult to sell.

♦ Develop a relationship with a jeweler you can trust. Then you won't have to worry about having unpleasant surprises when you have jewelry custom made.

136

14

How to Care for and Protect Your Diamond Ring

Cleaning Your Diamond Ring

W ould you like your diamond ring to look better than many rings that are far more valuable? There's a simple formula—keep it clean. A clean imperfect diamond, for example, can look more attractive than a dirty flawless diamond. Yet, there may be thousands of dollars of difference between the two.

It's hard, however, to keep a diamond ring clean. Diamonds are natural grease attractors. In fact, diamonds are separated from other stones and dirt by passing mined material over a grease belt. Diamonds stick to the grease while the other stones and dirt are washed away. Consequently, diamonds can become coated with grease when they are immersed in dishwater or when they come in contact with any greasy substance including lotions and natural skin oils.

A safe and easy way to clean a diamond ring is to soak and wash it in warm sudsy water using a mild liquid detergent. Then it can be dried with a soft, lint-free cloth. Ethyl alcohol, ammonia solutions and jewelry cleaning solutions may also be used for cleaning and soaking diamond jewelry. The alcohol has the advantage of evaporating quickly and not leaving water spots. Ammonia is not only good for cleaning unfilled diamonds; it's also good for brightening metals, particularly yellow gold. Alcohol and ammonia may damage other types of stones, so consult your jeweler before using them on anything but jewelry with unfilled diamonds. **Fracture-filled diamonds should not be cleaned in solutions which are acidic or which contain ammonia**. Such solutions could cause the fillings to gradually cloud, discolor or be removed.

Do not use chlorine solutions to clean rings. The chlorine can pit and dissolve gold alloys. This pitting can also occur when rings are worn while swimming.

If the dirt on the diamond(s) cannot be washed off with a cloth after soaking, try using a tooth pick, a Water Pick or unwaxed dental floss to remove caked-on dirt. Brushes should be used with caution because the bristles can scratch gold mountings.

Frequently, in order to get rid of encrusted dirt, rings must be cleaned professionally with steamers and ultrasonics (cleaning machines that can shake dirt loose with a vibrating detergent solution using high-frequency sound waves). Ultrasonic and steam cleaners should not be used for severely flawed or cracked diamonds or for gemstones such as opals, emeralds, pearls, coral, turquoise, malachite, tanzanite, moonstone and lapis lazuli.

Sometimes it takes hours to effectively clean a diamond ring in an ultrasonic. There are times, however, when ultrasonics and steamers cannot get rid of dirt and metal residue. In these cases, the diamonds may have to be boiled in sulfuric acid (fracture-filled diamonds should never be cleaned in acids). Lengthy and risky cleaning procedures can be avoided by cleaning jewelry on a regular basis. Once a week is not too often for a diamond ring that is worn daily.

Storing Your Diamond Ring

Protection from theft and damage should be prime considerations when storing a diamond ring. Jewelry boxes can protect a ring from damage if the ring is stored individually, but they are one of the first places burglars look when they break into a house. Therefore, it's best to reserve jewelry boxes for costume jewelry when they're displayed on tables or dressers.

Diamond rings should be wrapped separately in soft material or placed individually in pouches or the pockets of padded jewelry bags. If a diamond ring is placed next to or on top of other jewelry, the metal mountings or stones can get scratched. Use your imagination to find a secure place in your house to hide jewelry pouches, bags and boxes. If a ring is seldom worn, it's best to keep it in a safe deposit box.

Preventing Your Diamonds from Being Switched

Stone switching is less common than many people think, but it does occasionally occur. Wondering if a stone has been or will be switched can be just as disturbing as actually having it switched. Use the following guidelines to help avoid unnecessary worry or false accusations and to prevent your diamond(s) from being switched when you have it repaired or appraised.

◆ **Know your diamond(s).** What color is it approximately? What types of clarity characteristics does it have—chips, scratches, naturals, clouds, feathers? Where are these clarity characteristics located on the diamond? What type of girdle does it have—bruted, faceted or polished? Is the girdle thick or thin? Is the crown high or low? To determine these types of characteristics, no special instruments are needed except a loupe.

Diamond dealers and jewelers control stone switching by noting the weight, the measurements and the price of diamonds. Writing or drawing the clarity and cutting characteristics of diamonds would be too time-consuming. Lay people rarely have the scales and instruments needed to weigh and measure diamonds. They can, however, ask salespeople to write the weights on their sales receipts. The measurements of large diamonds can also be indicated. This information will then be available when needed.

◆ **Keep the diamond(s) clean.** This will help you recognize it. The color, clarity and brilliance of a dirty diamond can change so much when it is cleaned that the owner may not believe the stone is the same.

◆ **Have descriptive characteristics of your diamond(s) and ring written on both your copy and the store's copy of the take-in receipt.** If you leave a diamond bracelet or necklace with someone, also have the length of the piece and the number of stones or links written on the receipt. It's not uncommon for stores and appraisers to write *colorless stone* or *yellow metal* in place of *diamond* and *gold* if they don't have time to test the stone and the metal. Stores should, however, be willing to write down specific characteristics that are visible and measurable, if you ask them. Not only can written receipts serve as documentary evidence of switching, they can also help prevent it from occurring.

◆ **If you have a diagram or photograph of your diamond(s) or ring, photocopy it** and ask the store to acknowledge that it's a fair representation. The ring itself can also be photocopied.

◆ **Establish a relationship with a jeweler you feel is trustworthy.** This is probably the best preventative of all.

15

Tips on Smart Buying

If you've read and digested the material in this book, then you've taken a big step towards becoming a smart buyer. Despite your new-found knowledge, you'll need professional assistance. To determine if a salesperson is qualified to help you, I suggest you ask the two following questions when you're looking at rings and diamonds:

1. **How would you describe the quality of the cut of this diamond(s)?** Salespeople should be able to give you basic information about the proportioning of diamonds. For example, if a diamond has a very thin crown, competent salespeople should be able to tell you that the top of the stone is so thin it won't have much sparkle or fire. If a diamond has an extremely thick girdle, they should be able to point this out under magnification and explain that a well-cut diamond of the same weight would have a larger diameter and look more impressive. It's not sufficient for a salesperson to simply describe a diamond as a fine make or poor cut.

   It's helpful for salespeople to give you proportion measurements, but this is not essential nor always possible. What's more important is that the salesperson understand the significance of any measurements that may be known about a diamond.

   Any salesperson can read the clarity or color grade indicated on a diamond label or report. It requires skill, however, to provide information about cut quality just by looking at a diamond under magnification.

2. **Is this ring well crafted and able to withstand daily wear?** If yes, ask them to explain why. Knowledgeable salespeople will be able to show you under magnification good and/or bad features about the setting, finish and overall workmanship of the ring. They will also know which mountings and settings are more suited for everyday wear. Some are designed mainly for dressy occasions. And some are just designed as inexpensive costume-type jewelry.

In addition to asking the above questions, you should note the way salespeople deal with the subject of gem treatments. This not only indicates their competence, it provides clues about their ethics. They should be able to discuss treatments in plain language. Rather than just saying a stone is color or clarity enhanced, ethical salespeople will tell you if it's laser-drilled, irradiated, fracture-filled, or heat & pressure treated. And they will disclose and identify treatments voluntarily without your having to ask.

Here are some other shopping pointers:

♦ **Don't assume that a diamond with a brand name is better than a generic diamond.** It's become popular to inscribe brand names on the girdle of diamond as a marketing tool. Diamonds are valued on the basis of their inherent characteristics, not their brand name. In fact, none of the world's most noted and expensive diamonds are inscribed with brand names.

Any company can take diamonds of any quality and give them a brand name. One new ploy is to put an expensive-sounding brand name on treated diamonds to make them seem like they're really special to uneducated consumers.

◆ **Look at a range of qualities and styles** before buying diamonds and rings. This will give you a basis for comparison.

◆ **When judging prices, try to compare diamonds of the same shape, size, color, clarity and cut quality.** Compare mountings with the same metal type, weight, setting styles and workmanship. All of these factors affect the cost of a diamond ring. Because of the complexity of jewelry pricing, it's easiest for a lay person to compare diamonds or rings that are alike.

◆ **Compare per-carat diamond prices, not stone prices** (total cost of a diamond). Chapter 3 explains why.

◆ **Ask if the diamond(s) is untreated and natural.** A salesperson who claims a diamond is untreated should be willing to identify it as an untreated natural diamond on the sales receipt. Make this a condition of sale. If a salesperson says a diamond is enhanced or processed, then it's treated.

In some instances, you can save a lot of money by buying treated diamonds. However, for something as special as a wedding ring, it's advisable to get an untreated diamond.

If a jeweler or salesperson tells you they don't know if a diamond is treated, this is not a sign of incompetence. It's an indication of honesty. Treatments are now so sophisticated that trade members can't always be expected to be able to identify them. Jewelers usually assure themselves that their diamonds are untreated by sending them to specialized labs for examination and/or by purchasing them from sources that guarantee they're untreated.

◆ **Don't assume that all jewelers grade diamonds in the same way.** Some jewelers are more strict than others, so grades can be misleading. That's why it's important for you to understand how to judge diamond quality and to look at diamonds under magnification before buying them. Even diamonds accompanied by grading reports or certificates should be viewed carefully by the buyer. Many of these written evaluations, even from reputable labs, do not give a good description of the quality of the cut or the degree of brilliance.

◆ **Beware of sales or ads that seem too good to be true.** The advertised merchandise might be of unacceptable quality or it might have been stolen or misrepresented. Jewelers are in business to make money, not to lose it.

◆ **Be willing to compromise.** You'll probably have to do this in order to find a good buy and stay within your budget. Even people with unlimited budgets have to compromise sometimes on the size, shape, color or quality they want because of lack of availability. It's especially difficult to find fancy color diamonds of specific qualities and sizes. A diamond doesn't have to be perfect for you to enjoy it.

◆ **Make sure expensive diamonds are accompanied by a lab report.** It's not worth buying a lab report for a $200 diamond, but it is for a $2000 diamond. A lab report offers an independent assessment of the color, clarity and proportions of the stone, and it can protect you from ending up with a synthetic or treated diamond. For information on gem labs, appraisals, and lab reports, consult the *Gem & Jewelry Pocket Guide* by Renée Newman.

◆ **If possible, establish a relationship with a jeweler you can trust and who looks after your welfare.** He or she can help you find buys that you wouldn't find on your own.

◆ Look at the diamond(s) on your hand as it would normally be viewed and answer the following questions. (A negative answer to any one of the questions suggests the diamond is a poor choice).

   a. Is the diamond brilliant?

   b. Does it sparkle?

   c. Does it look good compared to other diamonds of the same shape and size? Keep in mind that lighting can affect the appearance of diamonds, so try to view them under different lights—fluorescent, daylight, spotlights, light bulbs and away from light.

◆ Put the ring on your finger and answer the following questions. (Again, a negative answer suggests the ring is a poor choice).

   a. Does it look good on your hand?

   b. Does it feel good on your hand?

   c. Is there a good chance that it will stay in style?

   d. Does it fit your personality?

   e. Is it practical for how you plan to wear it?

You might have expected the *Diamond Ring Buying Guide* to tell you what is the best diamond, metal and style for your ring. The fact is, however, there is no one diamond, metal or style for all people. Choosing a diamond ring is a very personal matter. The *Diamond Ring Buying Guide* was written to help you make your own buying decisions, not to dictate what you should buy.

When you get a diamond ring, you're getting more than just a rock attached to a hunk of metal. You're getting a work of art that you can hold and wear. You're getting a symbol of beauty, purity, strength and eternity. These symbolic associations are the result of the intrinsic characteristics of the ring materials.

Gold, platinum and diamonds have a lot in common. In their pure state, they're all composed of a single atomic element; they're all chemically stable and will not tarnish or change with time; they're all rare and can be used as ornaments or as a medium of exchange; they're all important to the health and welfare of modern man because of their technical and industrial applications; they've all played an important role in the history of mankind.

Before the 1700's, only kings, queens and other nobility were allowed to wear diamond rings. This is no longer an exclusive privilege. You can have the pleasure of wearing them and giving them as pledges of love and commitment. Your diamond ring is very special, just like the person wearing it. So treasure it; take good care of it. If you do, it can bring you and your loved ones years of enjoyment.

Suppliers of Jewelry & Diamonds for Photographs

Cover photo: Varna Platinum, Los Angeles, CA

Inside front cover photos: Top photo: Varna Platinum, Los Angeles, CA
    Bottom photo: Vivid Collection, New York, NY

Inside back cover photo: Wright & Lato, East Orange, NJ

Half-title page photo: Nagalle Designs, Wilsonville, OR

Photo facing title page: Wright & Lato, East Orange, NJ

Title page: Judith Conway, Windsor, CA

Chapter 1
Figs. 1.1, 1.2 & 1.7: J. Landau, Los Angeles, CA
Figs. 1.8 & 1.9: Josam Diamond Trading Corp., Los Angeles, CA

Chapter 2
Fig. 2.1: Natural rough. upper right: Ralph Shapiro, Los Angeles, CA
    octahedral diamond crystal, lower left: Rainbow G. I. Diamonds, Los Angeles, CA
Fig. 2.2: Asian Institute of Gemological Sciences, Bangkok, Thailand
Fig. 2.3: Todd Reed, Boulder, CO

Chapter 4
Figs. 4.1 & 4.27: Suberi Bros, New York, NY
Fig. 4.2: Global Diamonds, Inc., Chicago, IL
Figs. 4.3, 4.5, 4.10, 4.18, 4.23–4.26, 4.32–4.36: Josam Diamond Trading Corp., Los Angeles, CA
Figs. 4.8, 4.9, 4.17 & 4.37: Harry Winston Inc., New York, NY
Figs. 4.11, 4.12 & 4.19: Ebert & Company, Los Angeles, CA
Fig. 4.20: Andrew Sarosi, Los Angeles, CA
Fig. 4.22: Ambar Diamonds, Los Angeles, CA
Figs. 4.28 & 4.29: Christopher Designs, New York, NY
Fig. 4.30: Dr. Ulrich Freiesleben, Münster, Germany

Chapter 5
Figs. 5.1 & 5.2: Harry Winston, Inc. New York, NY
Fig. 5.3: Timeless Gem Designs, Los Angeles, CA
Fig. 5.4: Extrême Gioielli, Valenza, Italy
Fig. 5.5: Suberi Bros., New York, NY
Fig. 5.6: J. Landau Inc., Los Angeles, CA
Fig. 5.7: Eve J. Alfillé, Evanston, IL
Fig. 5.8: Sidney Mobell, San Francisco, CA
Figs. 5.9–5.11: Arthur Langerman, Antwerpen, Belgium
Fig. 5.12: Cynthia, Renée, Fallbrook, CA
Figs. 5.13 & 5.15: Vivid Collection, New York, NY

Chapter 6

Figs. 6.1, 6.3, 6.7 & 6.26: Josam Diamond Trading Corp., Los Angeles, CA
Figs. 6.5, 6.7 & 6.29: Suberi Bros., New York, NY
Figs. 6.27 & 6.28: J. Landau, Los Angeles, CA

Chapter 7

Figs. 7.3, 7.16–7.20, 7.25, 7.27–7.30: Josam Diamond Trading Corp., Los Angeles, CA
Fig. 7.26: J. Landau, Los Angeles, CA
Figs. 7.33–7.36: Lisa Poff, Los Angeles, CA

Chapter 8

Fig. 8.4: Varna Platinum, Los Angeles, CA

Chapter 9

Figs. 9.1 to 9.4: Yehuda Diamond Co. (Diascience Corp.), New York, NY

Chapter 10

Fig. 10.1: General Electric
Fig. 10.2: Alan Hodgkinson, Portencross by West Kilbride, Ayrshire, Scotland

Chapter 11

Fig. 11.1: Zsombor Antal, Newark, NJ
Fig. 11.2: Stuller, Lafayette, LA
Fig. 11.3: Scott Keating Designs, Basalt, CO
Fig. 11.4: Michael Bondanza, New York, NY
Fig. 11.5: Eve Alfillé, Evanston, IL
Fig. 11.6: Wade Miley Designer Jewelry; Gem Reflections, San Anselmo, CA
Fig. 11.7: Studio E, Edina, MN
Fig. 11.8: Michael Francis, Seattle. WA

Chapter 12

Figs. 12.1: Suberi Bros., New York, NY
Fig. 12.3: Mark Schneider, Long Beach, CA
Fig. 12.4: Gary Dulac Goldsmith, Vero Beach, FL
Figs. 12.5 & 12.9: Varna Platinum, Los Angeles, CA
Fig. 12.6: Michael Francis, Seattle, WA
Fig. 12.7: Wade Miley Designer Jewelry; Gem Reflections, San Anselmo, CA
Fig. 12.8: Nagalle Designs, Wilsonville, OR
Fig. 12.10: Stuller, Lafayette, LA
Figs. 12.11–12.13: Ambar Diamonds, Los Angeles, CA
Fig. 12.14: Peter Storm Designs, Belmont, CA
Fig. 12.15: Richard Kimball, Denver, CO

Chapter 13

Figs.13.2: Judith Conway, Windsor, CA
Fig. 13.3: Aaron Henry Designs, Los Angeles, CA
Fig. 13.4: Suna Bros., New York, NY
Fig. 13.5: Monile of Italy, Platinum Guild International, USA, Newport Beach, CA
Fig. 13.6: Varna Platinum, Los Angeles, CA
Figs. 13.7 & 13.9: Mark Schneider, Long Beach, CA
Fig. 13.8: Nagalle Designs, Wilsonville, OR
Fig. 13.10: Walls Design Ltd., Boulder, CO
Fig. 13.13: Richard Kimball, Denver, CO
Fig. 13.14: Zsombor Antal, Newark, NJ
Figs. 13.15 & 13.16: Gary Dulac Goldsmith, Vero Beach, FL

Chapter Quizzes

Chapter 3 Quiz (Carat Weight)

1. Is it possible for a 0.95 carat diamond to look bigger than a 1.05 carat diamond? Explain your answer.

2. What's a ten-pointer diamond?

3. When could a 1-carat cubic zirconia and a 1-carat diamond have the same measurements?

4. Which would probably be worth more: a 1-carat diamond solitaire ring or a cocktail ring with 20 diamonds having a total weight of 1.2 carats? (Assume that the color and quality of all the diamonds is the same.)

5. If a 2-carat diamond costs $8000, how much does it cost per carat?

6. How much does a 1/4 carat diamond cost if it sells for $1000 per carat?

7. Does a round-brilliant, 1-carat diamond always have a diameter of 6.5 mm?

Answers:

1. Yes. A 0.95 carat round diamond with a thin girdle can look bigger than a 1.05 carat round diamond with an extremely thick girdle and a high crown (top). A 0.95 carat triangular brilliant-cut diamond would tend to look bigger than a 1.05 carat round diamond.

2. A diamond that weighs 0.10 ct (1/10 of a carat).

3. Never, because of the diamond's lower density.

4. The 1-carat diamond solitaire ring would normally cost a lot more per carat.

5. $4000

$$\frac{\$8000}{2 \text{ ct}} = \$4000$$

6. $250

$$1/4 \times \$1000 = \$250$$

7. No. Its diameter will vary according to its proportions. 6.5 mm represents an average diameter for well-cut, round-brilliant diamonds weighing one carat.

Chapter 4 Quiz (Shape & Cutting Style)

Answer the Following Questions:

1. Which would normally cost more—a 1-carat round diamond or a 1-carat emerald-cut diamond (assume that the color and quality are the same)?

2. What is the bottom cone-shaped portion of a diamond called?

3. What is the name of the narrow rim around the circumference of the stone?

4. What is the large top facet of a stone called?

5. What is the top portion of the stone above the girdle called?

6. What is the difference between a brilliant-cut square and a step-cut square?

7. What are two other names for a brilliant-cut triangle.

Answers

1. The one-carat round diamond would normally cost more.
2. The pavilion
3. The girdle
4. The table
5. The crown
6. The brilliant-cut square would have triangular and kite-shaped facets that radiate from the center of the stone to the girdle. The step-cut square would have elongated, four-sided facets that are arranged in rows parallel to the girdle.
7. Trilliant and trillion. A *Trielle®* is a trillion made by the Trillion Diamond Co.

Chapter 5 Quiz (Judging Color)

Select the correct answer(s). **More than one answer may be possible** and therefore required.

1. Fancies are:
   a. Diamonds decorated with lace and sequins.
   b. Any shape diamond except round.
   c. Diamonds with a natural body color other than light yellow, light brown or light gray.
   d. Diamonds that have been artificially colored by irradiation and heat treatments.

2. A jeweler shows you a blue stone and identifies it as a diamond. The price seems very low for a blue diamond.
   a. You should assume that the jeweler doesn't know the difference between a sapphire and a diamond.
   b. You should buy it at once since the jeweler probably doesn't realize that naturally blue diamonds are very expensive.
   c. You should suspect that the stone has been artificially colored if it's a diamond.

3. You ask a jeweler you don't know to tell you what color the diamond in your yellow gold ring is. He tells you it's impossible for him to give you a precise color grade on the spot. This probably means that the jeweler:
   a. Doesn't know how to color grade diamonds.
   b. Feels that doctors and other professionals don't give out free services so why should he.
   c. Doesn't want to admit your diamond is a better color than anything he has in his store.
   d. Knows that your diamond should be examined out of its mounting with comparison stones for accurate color grading. Otherwise only an estimate grade can be given.

4. One of the jewelry stores in a local shopping mall is having a special diamond ring promotion. You are amazed at how much lower the prices are than the other stores in the same mall. You can assume that:
   a. There is a good chance that light brown or light yellow diamonds were used in the promotional rings.
   b. The more expensive jewelry stores are owned by a bunch of greedy crooks.
   c. The store with the lower prices will soon go out of business.

5. Which of the following can affect your perception of diamond color?
   a. The color of your clothes.
   b. The city you live in.
   c. The ten martinis you had the night before.
   d. The lighting.
   e. All of the above.

6. Becky wants a 1.00 carat D or E color diamond, and her jeweler tells her that he does not have any diamonds of that color and size in stock.
   a. She should assume that he only sells poor quality diamonds.
   b. She should ask if he can get a diamond that color and size.
   c. She should assume he has a very limited selection of diamonds

7. You're looking at a diamond ring and you note a distinct yellowish tint in the diamond. What is a possible color grade for the diamond?
   a. E
   b. H
   c. M
   d. S

8. Champagne diamonds
   a. Have an exotic, valuable color.
   b. Have a brownish tint.
   c. Cost less than near colorless diamonds.
   d. None of the above

Answers:
1. b and c,   2. c,   3. b and d,   4. a,   5. e,   6. b,   7. c and d   8. b and c.

Chapter 6 Quiz (Judging Cut)

True or False?

1. Diamonds of the same shape, color, clarity and carat weight always have the same value.

2. Diamonds with thin crowns and big tables generally have less sparkle and fire (flashes of rainbow colors) than those with higher crowns and smaller tables.

3. The term *cut* has a variety of meanings that apply to diamonds.

4. The brilliance of a diamond is determined only by its cut.

5. Extremely thick girdles can make diamonds appear small for their weight.

6. It's easy to find diamonds with perfect symmetry.

7. The diamond trade has no formal guidelines for determining exactly how the quality of the cut affects the price of a diamond.

8. Dark bowties increase the value of fancy-shaped diamonds.

9. The quality of the cut can play a large role in determining the value of a diamond.

10. A well-cut diamond can lack brilliance.

11. If a lab document says the polish and finish of a diamond is good, this means the diamond is well-proportioned.

12, A good way to shop for diamonds is to ask for example, "How much is a 1-carat, G-color, VS_2 diamond?"

Answers:

1. F The proportions and brilliance of a diamond also affect its value.
2. T
3. T
4. F A diamond's clarity, color and chemical composition also affect its brilliance.
5. T
6. F
7. T
8. F
9. T
10. T A well-cut diamond with low transparency and poor clarity can lack brilliance.
11. F Finish refers to the quality of just the surface of the stone. Even if the finish is good, the diamond may be poorly proportioned and lackluster.
12. F A question such as this would indicate that you are more interested in grades than diamond beauty. Salespeople might then take advantage of you by either misrepresenting the grades of their diamonds or by selling you a poorly cut stone that might be worth 30 to 40% less than a well-cut one.

   Instead of asking the price of a specific color and clarity grade, give salespeople an idea of the size, color and clarity range you are interested in and tell them you'd like a well-cut stone. Then when they show you the diamond(s), ask why they feel it's well-cut. Salespeople who are knowledgeable will be able to give specific reasons. They should also be able to compare it to one with a lower quality cut so you can see the difference.

Chapter 7 Quiz (Judging Clarity)

Select the correct answer.

1. When used for clarity grading, VS means:

    a. Vague scratches
    b. Various spots
    c. Very slightly included
    d. Very substandard

2. You're in a jewelry store and the owner asks to see your diamond ring. He places it under a microscope and tells you the diamond has a small crack in the center so it is a lousy diamond. When you look through the microscope, you are able to see a very small, fine line in the diamond. This means:

    a. Your diamond is defective.
    b. The diamond will soon crack into pieces.
    c. The owner is unprofessional, and he is giving you misleading information.
    d. The owner is a true diamond expert and deserves your patronage.

3. You want to sell an old diamond ring. The total weight of the diamonds is four carats. You ask a jeweler how much she will pay you for it, but she says she can't give you a price until the ring is cleaned. This means:

    a. The jeweler does not want to buy the ring.
    b. The jeweler wants to embarrass you.
    c. Your ring is so valuable that the jeweler can't afford to buy it; and even if she could, her clientele probably wouldn't be able to afford it.
    d. The jeweler knows that the color and clarity of diamonds cannot be accurately determined unless the stones are clean; and without this information, it's not possible to determine the value.

4. Your boyfriend gives you a diamond for your birthday. When you look at it with a loupe, you can easily see some black spots in the center of the diamond. You can't see them or any other blemishes or inclusions with your naked eye. This means:

    a. Your diamond is worthless and your boyfriend is cheap.
    b. It's possible that your diamond has a clarity grade of SI_2.
    c. It's possible that your diamond has a clarity grade of VVS_2.
    d. Your diamond is tainted with coal particles.

5. Which of the following clarity features is **least** likely to affect the clarity grade of a diamond.

    a. naturals
    b. clouds
    c. feathers
    d. crystals

6. You're looking at a diamond, and you can see white spots in it with your naked eye. What is a possible clarity grade for the diamond?

   a. VVS_1
   b. VS_2
   c. IF
   d. I_2

7. You have a friend that claims to be a gemologist. When you ask him to estimate the clarity grade of the diamond in a solitaire ring you just bought, he hesitates and says that it looks like it's at least an SI. You should assume that:

   a. Your friend is either an incompetent gemologist or not one at all since he can't give you a clear-cut answer.
   b. Your friend is embarrassed to tell you the true clarity grade of the diamond because he doesn't want to hurt your feelings or imply that your jeweler sold you a poor diamond.
   c. Your friend's eyesight is probably failing.
   d. Your friend knows it's difficult to assign clarity grades to diamonds set in rings because the settings can hide clarity characteristics, especially when the clarity grades are potentially high.

8. Which of the following statements is **false**?

   a. A difference of one or two clarity grades can sometimes affect the value of a diamond by thousands of dollars.
   b. It is normal for diamonds to have blemishes and inclusions.
   c. There are no advantages to buying a diamond with inclusions and blemishes.
   d. It's possible for an I_1 diamond that's mounted in a ring to look better than an SI_2 diamond.

Answers:
1. c,   2. c,   3. d,   4. b,   5. a,   6. d,   7. d,   8. c.

Chapter 11 Quiz (Gold & Platinum)

Select the correct answer(s). **More than one answer may be possible and therefore required.**

1. You have a 14K yellow gold ring that discolors very easily. What does this indicate?
   a. The ring is not gold, because gold does not tarnish.
   b. You do not know how to take care of jewelry.
   c. The 14K gold alloy may contain a high percentage of copper.
   d. You have a cheap ring.

2. 18K gold is:
   a. 18/100 gold
   b. 90% gold
   c. 3/4 gold
   d. 1/18 gold

3. In terms of actual gold value, which of the following rings is the best value if their price is the same?

   a. 14K ring weighing 5 grams.
   b. 18K ring weighing 5 grams.
   c. 14K ring weighing 5 pennyweight.
   d. 18k ring weighing 5 pennyweight.

4. You have an E color diamond and you would like to emphasize its lack of color. Which type of mountings would be most appropriate?

   a. A white gold mounting.
   b. A platinum mounting.
   c. A mounting entirely of yellow gold.

5. White gold is:

   a. A special variety of gold found only in certain mines of South Africa and Canada.
   b. Gold alloyed with aluminum.
   c. Gold to which bleach has been added.
   d. None of the above.

6. An 18K gold solitaire ring set with a five-carat diamond weighs six grams. What is the value of the gold if the spot price of gold is $500 per ounce.

   a. $60
   b. $65.63
   c. $72
   d. $80

7. You see *583* stamped on the inside of a ring. This number means:

   a. The ring should be 14K gold.
   b. The price of the ring is $583.
   c. The ring weighs 0.583 oz t.
   d. The ring should contain about 58% gold and 42% other metals.

8. An 18K gold bracelet weighs 1 ounce on a postage scale, one used for weighing letters. The spot price of gold is $400 an ounce. What is the value of the gold in the bracelet?

   a. $400
   b. $364.40
   c. $300
   d. $273.30

Answers

1. c
2. c

3. d. A pennyweight is 1.555 times heavier than a gram and 18K has a higher percentage of gold than 14K.

4. a or b

5. d. White gold is typically made by alloying yellow gold with palladium or copper, zinc and nickel. Aluminum is not used.

6. a. The diamond in the ring weighs five carats which equals 1 gram. This means the ring mounting by itself weighs 5 grams. 1 gram = 0.032 oz t, so the mounting, which weighs 5 grams = .16 oz t. Pure gold is $500 an ounce. (Remember, the weight of gold is always quoted in troy ounces). Therefore, the gold value of 18K (75%) is $375 an ounce. $375 x .16 oz t = $60

7. a and d

8. d. Remember the ounce on a postal scale is different than the ounce on a gold scale. Therefore, you'll have to convert the weight to troy ounces. 1 oz av = .911 oz t so the bracelet weighs .911 oz t. If gold is $400 an ounce, then the gold in 18K gold is worth $300 an ounce. $300 x .911 oz t = $273.30

True or False?

1. Platinum is an ideal metal for mounting colorless diamonds.

2. Before World War II, white gold was the most preferred white metal.

3. Platinum is less expensive than white gold.

4. The marking "950 PT" indicates the metal is 95% platinum.

5. Platinum is about twice as heavy as silver.

6. Gold holds diamonds more securely than platinum.

7. Platinum is used to mask the color of yellowish diamonds.

8. Platinum is an excellent alternative for people who are allergic to gold alloys.

9. Platinum is harder and more durable than gold.

10. Rhodium is commonly used to plate white gold.

11. Gold rings are never made with platinum prongs because it's impossible to solder the two metals together due to their different melting temperatures.

12. Neither pure gold nor platinum will tarnish.

Answers

1. T, 2. F, 3. F, 4. T, 5. T, 6. F, 7. F, 8. T, 9. T, 10. T, 11. F, 12. T.

Bibliography

Diamonds

Argenzio, Victor. *Diamonds Eternal*. New York: David McKay, 1974.

Balfour, Ian. *Famous Diamonds*. London: Collins, 1987

Blakey, George. *The Diamond*. New York: Paddington Press, 1977.

Bruton, Eric. *Diamonds*. Radnor, PA: Chilton, 1978.

Cuellar, Fred. *How to Buy a Diamond*. Naperville, IL: Casablanca Press, 2000.

Dickinson, Joan Younger. *The Book of Diamonds*. New York: Crown Publishers, 1965.

Friedman, Michael. *The Diamond Book*. Homewood, IL: Dow Jones-Irwin, 1980.

Gemological Institute of America. Diamond Course
Gemological Institute of America. *The GIA Diamond Dictionary*. Santa Monica, CA: GIA, 1993.

Green, Timothy. *The World of Diamonds*. New York: William Morrow, 1981.

Hofer, Stephen C. *Collecting & Classifying Coloured Diamonds*. New York: Ashland Press, 1998.

Koivula, John. *The Microworld of Diamonds*. Northbrook, IL: Gemworld International Inc., 2000.

Kassoy Inc. *Everything You Always Wanted to Know about Diamonds*. New York: Kassoy Inc., 1977.

Pagel-Theisen, Verena. *Diamond Grading ABC*. New York: Rubin & Son, 1986.

Roskin, Gary. *Photo Masters For Diamond Grading*. Northbrook, IL: Gemworld International, 1994.

Spero, Saul A. *Diamonds, Love, & Compatibility*. Hicksville, NY: Exposition Press, 1977.

Vleeschdrager, Eddy. *Dureté 10: Le diamant, 3 édition, histoire-taille-commerce*. Deurne (Anvers): 1996.

Gold & Platinum

Branson, Oscar T. *What You Need to Know About Your Gold and Silver*. Tucson, AZ: Treasure Chest Publications, 1980.

Brod, I. Jack. *Consumer's Guide to Buying and Selling Gold, Silver, and Diamonds*. Garden City, NY: Doubleday, 1985.

Burkett, Russell. *Everything You Wanted to Know about Gold and Other Precious Metals*. Whittier, CA: Gem Guides Book Co., 1975.

Cavelti, Peter C. *New Profits in Gold, Silver & Strategic Metals*. New York: McGraw-Hill, 1985.

Knuth, Bruce. *Jeweler's Resource, A reference of Gems, Metals, Formulas and Terminolgy for Jewelers*. Thornton, CO: Jewelers Press, 1994.

Merton, Henry A. *Your Gold & Silver*. New York: Macmillan, 1981.

Smith, Ernest A. *Working in Precious Metals*. Colchester, Essex: N.A.G. Press Ltd., 1991.

Sutherland, C. H. V. *Gold Its Beauty, Power and Allure*. New York: McGraw-Hill, 1969.

Jewelry and Gems

AGTA, *1997-98 Source Directory* & Gemstone Enhancement Information Chart.

Carmona, Charles. *The Complete Handbook for Gemstone Weight Estimation*. Los Angeles: Gemania Publishing, 1998.

Cologni, Franco & Nussbaum, Eric. *Platinum by Cartier*. Harry N. Abrams. 1996.

Dennis, Daniel J. *Gems: A lively Guide for the Casual Collector*. New York: Harry N Abrams, 1999.

Gemological Institute of America. Appraisal Seminar handbook.
Gemological Institute of America. Gem Identification Course.
Gemological Institute of America. Jewelry Repair Workbook.
Gemological Institute of America. Jewelry Sales Course.

Geolat, Patti, Van Northrup, C., Federman, David. *The Professional's Guide to Jewelry Insurance Appraising*. Shawnee Mission, KS: Modern Jeweler, 1994.

Gemological Institute of America. *Gem Reference Guide*. Santa Monica, CA: GIA, 1988.

Gubelin, Eduard & Franz-Xavier, Erni. *Gemstones: Symbols of Beauty and Power*. Lucerne: EMB Service for Publishers, 2000.

Hanneman, Wm. *Guide to Affordable Gemology*. Poulsbo, WA: Hanneman Gemological Instruments, 1998.

Hodgkinson, Alan. *Visual Optics: The Hodgkinson Method*. Gemworld Intl. Inc., Northbrook, IL, 1995.

Hughes, Richard W. *Ruby & Sapphire*. Boulder, CO: RWH Publishing, 1997.

Jarvis, Charles A. *Jewelry Manufacture and Repair*. New York: Bonanza, 1979.

Liddicoat, Richard T. *Handbook of Gem Identification*. Santa Monica, CA: GIA, 1993.

Maerz, Jurgen. "Platinum Alloys and Their Application in Jewelry Making:" Newport: PGI USA, 1999.

Marcum, David. *Fine Gems and Jewelry*. Homewood, IL.: Dow Jones-Irwin, 1986.

Matlins, Antoinette L. & Bonanno, A. C. *Engagement & Wedding Rings*. South Woodstock, VT: Gemstone Press, 1999.

McCreight, Tim. *Jewelry: Fundamentals of Metalsmithing*. Madison, WI: Hand Books Press, 1997.
McCreight, Tim. *The Complete Metalsmith*. Worcester, MA: Davis Publications, 1991

Miller, Anna M. *Gems and Jewelry Appraising*. New York: Van Nostrand Reinhold Company, 1988.

Morton, Philip. *Contemporary Jewelry*. New York: Holt, Rinehart, and Winston, 1976.

Nassau, Kurt. *Gems Made by Man*. Santa Monica, CA. Gemological Institute of America, 1980.
Nassau, Kurt. *Gemstone Enhancement*, Second Edition. London: Butterworths, 1994.

O'Donoghue, Michael. *Synthetic, Imitation & Treated Gemstones*. Oxford: Butterworth-Heinemann,1997.

Pinton, Diego. *Jewellery Technology*. Milan: Edizioni Gold Sri, 1999.

Preston, William S. *Guides for the Jewelry Industry*. New York: Jewelers Vigilance Committee, Inc., 1986.

Ramsey, John L. & Ramsey, Laura J. *The Collector/Investor Handbook of Gems*. San Diego, CA: Boa Vista Press, 1994.

Revere, Alan, *Professional Goldsmithing*. New York: Van Nostrand Reinhold, 1991.

Sarett, Morton R. *The Jewelry in Your Life*. Chicago: Nelson-Hall, 1979.

Schiffer, Nancy N. *Before you Buy an Engagement Ring*. Atglen, PA: Schiffer Publishing, 1999.

Schumann, Walter. *Gemstones of the World: Revised & Expanded Edition*. New York: Sterling 1997.

Sprintzen, Alice. *Jewelry: Basic Techniques and Design*. Radnor, PA: Chilton, 1980

SSEF Swiss Gemmological Institute. *Standards & Applications for Diamond Report,, Gemstone Report, Test Report.*.Basel: SSEF Swiss Gemmological Institute, 1998.

Stuller. *The Mountings Book, Volume 22*. Lafayette, LA: Stuller Setting's Inc, 1999.

Suwa, Yasukazu. *Gemstones: Quality and Value* (English Edition). Santa Monica, CA: Gemological Institute of America & Suwa & Son, 1994.

Suwa, Yasukazu. *Gemstones: Quality and Value Volume 2*. Tokyo: Sekai Bunka-sha, 1998.

Untracht, Oppi. *Jewelry Concepts & Technology*. New York: Doubleday, 1982.

Von Neumann, Robert. *The Design and Creation of Jewelry*. Radnor, PA: Chilton, 1972.

Wykoff, Gerald L. *Beyond the Glitter*. Washington DC: Adamas, 1982.

Periodicals & Miscellaneous

American Jewelry Manufacturer. Philadelphia, PA.

Auction Market Resource for Gems & Jewelry. P. O. Box 7683, Rego Park, NY 11374.

Australian Gemmologist. Brisbane: Gemmological Association of Australia

Deljanin, Branko & Sherman, Gregory. *Changing the Color of Diamonds: The High Pressure High Temperature Process Explained*. New York: EGL USA, 2000.

Gems and Gemology. Carlsbad, CA: Gemological Institute of America.

The Goldsmith. Atlanta, GA: Allen/Abernathy Division of A/S/M Communications Inc.

The Guide. Northbrook, IL: Gemworld International Inc. 1999 & 2000.

Jewelers Circular Keystone. Radnor, PA: Chilton Publishing Co.

Jewelers' Quarterly Magazine. Sonoma, CA.

Journal of Gemology, London: Gemological Association and Gem Testing Laboratory of Great Britain.

Modern Jeweler. Lincolnshire, IL: Vance Publishing Inc.

National Jeweler. New York: Gralla Publications.

New York Diamonds. New York: International Diamond Publications, Ltd.

Professional Jeweler. Philadelphia: Bond Communications.

Rapaport Diamond Report. New York: Rapaport Corp.

Science, Vol. 234. "Is Diamond the New Wonder Material?" Nov. 28, 1986.

Science News, Vol. 130. "Diamond Electronics: Sparkling Potential." Aug. 23, 1986.

Sky & Telescope. "Stardust on Earth." June 1987.

Index

Order Form

TITLE	Price Each	Quantity	Total
Diamond Ring Buying Guide, 6th Edition	$17.95		
Pearl Buying Guide	$19.95		
Ruby, Sapphire & Emerald Buying Guide	$19.95		
Gold & Platinum Jewelry Buying Guide	$19.95		
Gemstone Buying Guide	$19.95		
Gem & Jewelry Pocket Guide	$11.95		
Book Total			
SALES TAX for California residents only (book total x $.08)			
SHIPPING: USA: first book $2.00, each additional copy $1.25 Canada & foreign - surface mail: first book $3.50 ea. addl. $2.00 Canada & Mexico - airmail: first book $6.00, ea. addl. $3.50 All other foreign destinations - airmail: first book $11.00, ea. addl. $7.00			
TOTAL AMOUNT with tax (if applicable) and shipping (Pay foreign orders with an international money order or a check drawn on a U.S. bank.) **TOTAL**			

Mail check or money order in U.S. funds

To: International Jewelry Publications
P.O. Box 13384
Los Angeles, CA 90013-0384 USA

Ship to:

Name_____

Address_____

City_____ State or Province_____

Postal or Zip Code_____ Country _____

OTHER PUBLICATIONS BY RENEE NEWMAN

Pearl Buying Guide

"**If you're thinking of investing in pearls, invest $20 first in the** *Pearl Buying Guide*...Even if you already own pearls, this book has good tips on care and great ideas on ways to wear pearls."
San Jose Mercury News

"...An indispensable guide to judging [pearl] characteristics, distinguishing genuine from imitation, and making wise choices...useful to all types of readers, from the professional jeweler to the average patron... **highly recommended"**
Library Journal

"**An easily read, interesting, and helpful book on pearls**...This book would be a good starting place for a jewellery clerk wanting to improve his or her salesmanship, and would even be a help for a graduate gemmologist seeking a better understanding of what to look for when examining or appraising a pearl necklace."
The Canadian Gemmologist

"**A gem-dandy guide to picking right-price pearls."**
Boston Herald

156 pages, 111 color and 40 black/white photos, 7" by 9", ISBN 0-929975-27-8, $19.95 US

Gemstone Buying Guide

A **full-color**, comprehensive guide to evaluating, identifying, selecting and caring for colored gems.

"**A quality Buying Guide** that is recommended for purchase to consumers, gemmologists and students of gemmology—irrespective of their standard of knowledge of gemmology. The information is comprehensive, factual, and well presented. Particularly noteworthy in this book are the 189 quality colour photographs that have been carefully chosen to illustrate the text."
Australian Gemmologist

"**Praiseworthy**, a beautiful gem-pictorial reference and a help to everyone in viewing colored stones as a gemologist or gem dealer would...One of the finest collections of gem photographs I've ever seen...If you see the book, you will probably purchase it on the spot."
Anglic Gemcutter

"**Excellent illustrations**...certainly successful. It is worth having for both novices and more experienced lapidaries and gem buyers."
Lapidary Journal

"**Beautifully produced**...With colour on almost every opening, few could resist this book whether or not were they were in the gem and jewellery trade. The book should be on the counter or by the bedside (or both)."
Journal of Gemmology

152 pages, 189 color photos, 7" X 9", $19.95 US

Ruby, Sapphire & Emerald Buying Guide
How to Evaluate, Identify, Select & Care for These Gemstones

"**The best produced book on gemstones I have yet seen in this price range** (how is it done?). This is the book for anyone who buys, sells or studies gemstones. This style of book (and similar ones by the same author) is the only one I know which introduces actual trade conditions and successfully combines a good deal of gemmology with them...**Buy it, read it, keep it.**"
  Michael O'Donoghue, *Journal of Gemmology*

"**Solid, informative and comprehensive**...dissects each aspect of ruby and sapphire value in detail... a wealth of grading information...a definite thumbs-up. There is something here for everyone."
  C. R. Beesley, President, American Gemological Laboratories. *Jewelers' Circular Keystone*

164 pages, 175 color and 21 black/white photos, 7" by 9", ISBN 0-929975-28-6, $19.95 US

Gold & Platinum Jewelry Buying Guide
How to Judge, Buy, Test & Care for It

"**This book should be required reading for consumers and jewelers alike!** It offers step-by-step instructions for how to examine and judge the quality of craftsmanship and materials even if you know nothing about jewelry. If you are thinking of buying, making or selling jewelry as a hobby, as a career or just one time, then this book is a great place to start."
  Alan Revere, master goldsmith and director of the Revere Academy of Jewelry Arts

"**Enjoyable reading...profusely illustrated with color photographs** showing not only the beauty of finished jewelry but close-ups and magnification of details such as finish, settings, flaws and fakes.. sophisticated enough for professionals to use...highly recommended... **Newman's guides are the ones to take along when shopping.**"
  Library Journal

156 pages, 127 color & 67 black/white photos, 6 3/4" by 9", ISBN 0-929975-29-4, $19.95 US

Gem & Jewelry Pocket Guide
A traveler's guide to buying diamonds, colored gems, pearls, gold and platinum jewelry

"**Brilliantly planned, painstakingly researched, and beautifully produced**...this handy little book comes closer to covering all of the important bases than any similar guides have managed to do. From good descriptions of the most popular gem materials (plus gold and platinum), to jewelry craftsmanship, treatments, gem sources, appraisals, documentation, and even information about U.S. customs for foreign travelers—it is all here. I heartily endorse this wonderful pocket guide."
  John S. White, former Curator of Gems & Minerals at the Smithsonian Institution, *Lapidary Journal*

"**Short guides don't come better than this**...As always with this author, the presentation is immaculate and each opening displays high-class pictures of gemstones and jewellery."
  Michael O'Donoghue, *Journal of Gemmology*.

156 pages, 108 color photos, 4 1/2" by 7", ISBN 0-929975-30-8, $11.95 US

Available at bookstores, jewelry supply stores, the GIA or by mail: See reverse side for order form.

Order Form

TITLE	Price Each	Quantity	Total
Diamond Ring Buying Guide, 6th Edition	$17.95		
Pearl Buying Guide	$19.95		
Ruby, Sapphire & Emerald Buying Guide	$19.95		
Gold & Platinum Jewelry Buying Guide	$19.95		
Gemstone Buying Guide	$19.95		
Gem & Jewelry Pocket Guide	$11.95		
		Book Total	
SALES TAX for California residents only	(book total x $.08)		
SHIPPING: USA: first book $2.00, each additional copy $1.25 Canada & foreign - surface mail: first book $3.50 ea. addl. $2.00 Canada & Mexico - airmail: first book $6.00, ea. addl. $3.50 All other foreign destinations - airmail: first book $11.00, ea. addl. $7.00			
TOTAL AMOUNT with tax (if applicable) and shipping (Pay foreign orders with an international money order or a check drawn on a U.S. bank.)		**TOTAL**	

Mail check or money order in U.S. funds

To: International Jewelry Publications
P.O. Box 13384
Los Angeles, CA 90013-0384 USA

Ship to:

Name_____

Address_____

City_____ State or Province_____

Postal or Zip Code_____ Country _____